TORTILLA
— Lovers —
Cook Book

by

Bruce *and* ***Bobbi Fischer***

GOLDEN WEST ☼ PUBLISHERS

Also by Bruce and Bobbi Fischer:

> *Cowboy Cook Book*
> *Grand Canyon Cookbook*
> *Utah Cook Book*
> *Western Breakfast and Brunch Recipes*

CREDITS, ACKNOWLEDGMENTS

Piña Quesadillas: Dole Food Company, 5795 Lindero Canyon Rd., Westlake Village, CA 91352.

Charlie Brown's Mexican Roll-ups: Mabel Keithley, aka Charlie Brown, Phoenix, Arizona.

Sandi's Chicken Burritos Enchilada Style, Red Chile Sauce: Sandra Nickler from The Arizona Brand Food Company, Phoenix, Arizona.

Taco de Gallina, Bueno Taco Sauce, Bueno Burrito: Bueno Food Products, P.O. Box 293, Albuquerque, NM 87103

Sherry's Zesty Cheese Enchiladas: Sherry Potter, Scottsdale, Arizona.

Mabel's Magnificent Green Chile Burros: Mabel Keithley, Phoenix, Arizona.

Library of Congress Cataloging-in-Publication Data

Fischer, Bruce
    Tortilla Lovers Cook Book / by Bruce Fischer & Bobbi Salts
       p. cm.
    Includes index.
    1. Tortillas   I. Salts, Roberta II.   Title:
    TX770.T65F57 1996   96-15425
    641.8' 15—dc20   CIP

Printed in the United States of America

15th Printing © 2005

ISBN #1-885590-13-X

Golden West Publishers, Inc.
4113 N. Longview Ave.
Phoenix, AZ 85014, USA
800-658-5830

For free sample recipes and complete Table of Contents for every Golden West cookbook, visit: **goldenwestpublishers.com**

Table of Contents

Tantalizing Tortillas

Appetizers

Breakfasts

Soups & Salads

Main Dishes

Tortilla Treats

Introduction

The tortilla has had an illustrious history.

The tortilla, a flat corn pancake, was a staple of many native North American diets for centuries.

When the Spaniards arrived in the New World in search of wealth and conquest they introduced many new products to the native diet, including wheat. They shared their knowledge of growing, harvesting and milling the new food. The tortilla became the dietary foundation for new and native peoples. And the cultures merged.

Today, we have a choice between two basic types of tortillas—flour and corn. More recently, whole wheat and blue-corn tortillas have gained in popularity. Such newcomers as green chile, blue-berry and chocolate tortillas have emerged as added culinary delights.

The corn tortilla still accompanies most Mexican meals. You can serve it flat, rolled, fried, baked, folded, stacked, wet or dry, plain, stuffed with ingredients or topped with sauces. Today, there are no limits when creating tantalizing tortillas for any feast. Tortilla creations vary, from tacos and burros to enchiladas and tostadas and from quesadillas and flautas to chimichangas and burritos.

Tortilla Lovers Cook Book is a collection of savory, Southwestern dishes featuring the tortilla prepared in a variety of ways to satisfy the most discriminating tortilla lover's tastes. You will find traditional recipes that have their roots in Mexico and the American Southwest. Other tortilla recipes have been adapted to meet today's contemporary life-styles and preferences.

In the traditional method of preparing **corn tortillas,** dried corn kernels were simmered in lime and water until softened (called *nixtamal*). A stone mortar (*metaté*) and pestle (*mono*) were used to hand grind the corn. Once ground, the meal was moistened with water to create a fresh, smooth dough (*masa*).

As the native cooks handled the masa, they formed it into small balls. Then, with moistened palms, they patted the balls into thin

pancakes which were cooked on a lime-coated grill or metal griddle called a *comal*.

This process released locked proteins and minerals from the dry corn kernels. The flavor of fresh masa is unforgettable. It is similar in taste to grilled corn on the cob; some compare it to savoring the most exquisite, freshly-made, buttery popcorn. The ancient method of preparing corn tortillas is still practiced in some rural areas of Mexico today!

If you wish to make your own masa, you may do so by purchasing *masa harina*—a parched, ground corn flour treated with lime, produced by Quaker® and widely distributed. By simply adding water and a little salt to taste, you can make fresh masa to create delicious corn tortillas (see page 11).

Today, packaged corn tortillas are available in most grocery stores. Keep corn tortillas in the refrigerator for approximately 3-5 days, but don't freeze them because they will not soften after initial hardening. When purchasing packaged corn tortillas, look for ones that are soft and fairly pliable, whitish in color and even-textured. You should be able to detect a fresh corn aroma.

The early Spanish settlers imported the first **flour tortillas** from the northern part of Mexico into the Southwest. These tortillas were easy to make and cooked well on a hot griddle over an open campfire. Lard, made from pork fat, was used for cooking. Today, you can substitute margarine, vegetable oil, canola oil or butter for the lard.

You can make your own flour tortillas (see page 10) or purchase packaged ones from your grocer. Flour tortillas store well in the refrigerator, lasting a week or more. They also do well when frozen for lasting freshness.

Flour tortillas are kneaded on a lightly floured board. After the thin, round pancakes are formed, they are cooked on a hot, ungreased surface. (Some cooks prefer a lightly greased surface.)

Packaged flour tortillas come in many sizes ranging from 6 to 12 and, even, 18 inches. Most standard recipes call for burrito size, or 10-inch, tortillas. Look for those that are fresh, soft-textured and smooth.

Tortilla Tips

Tortillas are tastier when they are warm, soft, moist and pliable. To achieve this, you can steam them or warm them in the oven, microwave, ungreased griddle, skillet or barbeque grill.

To **steam** tortillas, place them in a steamer basket above hot water for a few seconds on each side. Remove them from the basket when they are soft and pliable. Be careful, if left to steam too long, the tortillas will fall apart.

For **oven** warming, wrap tortillas in aluminum foil and place them in a pre-heated 350° oven for 10 minutes or until warm.

To warm tortillas in a **microwave**, simply place a moist paper towel between each tortilla as you stack them on a microwave safe dish. Heat on high for approximately 6-8 seconds.

To heat tortillas on an **ungreased griddle**, or **skillet**, place each tortilla, one at a time, on pre-heated cooking surface using medium-high heat. Turn while warming for approximately 30 seconds.

Try a **barbeque grill** to add a smoked flavor to tortillas. Lay tortillas flat on the grill surface for a few seconds, flip and quickly remove from the heat. The temperature of the coals and the distance from the grill will determine just how long to keep tortillas heating.

To **soften** corn tortillas, place them one at a time in 1/2" of hot cooking oil for a few seconds. Turn and remove after a few more seconds. Place on a paper towel to drain. Be careful not to allow tortilla to get hard or brown.

Tortilla Terminology

Burro—a warmed, soft flour tortilla folded and filled with beans, meat, chicken, etc.

Burrito—a small burro.

Chimichanga—a flour tortilla, filled, folded on four sides and deep fried.

Enchilada—a soft, filled corn tortilla covered with a sauce and topped with cheese. (Usually baked.)

Enchilada Style—an entrée covered with sauce and cheese.

Fajitas—marinated strips of beef, chicken or vegetables that are grilled or broiled and served with a flour tortilla and savory fillings.

Flauta—a corn tortilla, rolled tightly and deep-fried.

Gorditas—thick flour tortillas popular in the Southwest.

Masa—fresh corn dough.

Masa Harina—commercially prepared corn flour.

Nachos—corn tortilla chips covered with cheese and other toppings and heated until cheese melts. Serve with sour cream, salsa and guacamole.

Quesadillas—a tortilla topped with cheese and heated or crisped until cheese is melted. Served flat or folded.

Taco—a soft or crisp tortilla, folded in half, and filled.

Tortilla—a thin flat, pancake made of corn or flour.

Tostada—a flat corn tortilla with various toppings

Flour Tortillas

6 1/2 cups FLOUR
2 Tbsp. BAKING POWDER
1 Tbsp. SALT
1/2 cup VEGETABLE SHORTENING
2 cups (approx.) LUKEWARM WATER

1.) Mix flour, baking powder, salt and shortening by hand until mixture becomes coarse in texture. Add water a little at a time. Mix until dough pulls away from sides of bowl without sticking. Knead about 30-40 times.

2.) Shape into balls (approximately 2").

3.) Grease hands with shortening (1/2 tsp.) and rub on balls to prevent crust from forming.

4.) Cover with a towel and let sit for ten minutes. Sprinkle board or hard surface lightly with flour.

5.) Roll dough balls with rolling pin into a circle about 10" across and 1/8" thick. Heat tortillas in hot skillet. When tortillas form light brown bubbles (blisters), turn and cook the other side.

Makes 20-24 (10") tortillas.

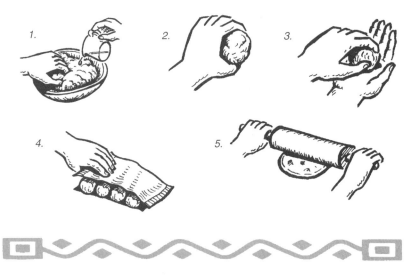

Corn Tortillas

2 cups CORN FLOUR (MASA HARINA)
1/2 tsp. SALT
1 1/4 cup WARM WATER

1.) Mix masa harina and salt together in a bowl. Add 1 cup of water, a little at a time, as you continue to mix ingredients. Knead dough, adding more water, if necessary. Dough must hold its shape and stay moist. Let rest 25-30 minutes.

2.) Divide into twelve balls each the size of a medium egg.

3.) Press and pat balls into tortilla shape or use tortilla press.

Place tortilla on ungreased hot griddle and cook until golden brown. When bubbling stops, turn and brown other side. Remove from griddle while tortilla is pliable. Stack tortillas to keep moist and warm. Use immediately or allow to cool. Place in airtight container and refrigerate for future use. Reheat before serving.

Makes 12 (6") tortillas.

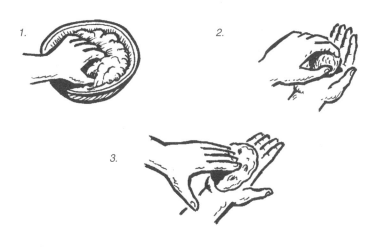

Folding Tortillas

Once you have created a mouth-watering filling, it is very tempting to stuff a tortilla with as much as you think it will hold. However, as tempting as it is, the secret in making a non-messy burrito or other tortilla meal is to keep from over-filling your tortilla.

Follow the diagram below to fold a tortilla.

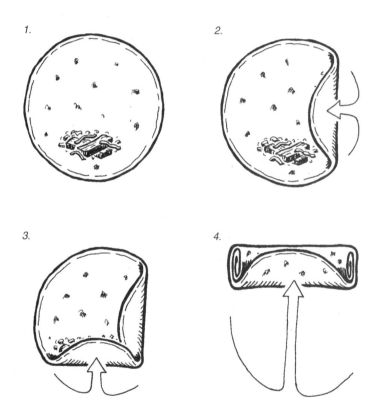

Tantalizing Tortillas

Healthy Heart Tortillas

A great tortilla recipe for today's healthy lifestyle.

6 cups FLOUR
1 tsp. BAKING POWDER
1 tsp. SALT
1/2 cup CORN OIL
2 cups WARM WATER

Mix dry ingredients together in a bowl. Add oil and blend. Slowly add 1 1/2 cups of warm water. Mix well. Dough should be smooth and pliable. If dough is too dry, add more water and knead dough. Make into balls about the size of a medium egg. Rub each ball with oil and cover. Let sit 15-20 minutes. Roll with a rolling pin to 8" diameter. Lightly brown on a hot griddle until bubbly. Turn once and lightly brown the other side.

Makes 1 1/2 dozen.

Green Chile Tortillas

3 cups FLOUR
1/2 tsp. BAKING POWDER
1/2 tsp. SALT
1 Tbsp. BLACK PEPPER
1 tsp. GARLIC SALT

1 can (4 oz.) GREEN CHILES,
    chopped
1/4 cup CORN OIL
1 cup WARM WATER

Mix dry ingredients together in a bowl and stir. Add green chiles and oil and blend. Slowly add 1 cup of warm water. Mix well. Dough should be smooth and pliable. If dough is too dry, add more water and knead dough. Make into balls about the size of a small-medium egg. Rub each ball with oil and cover with towel. Let sit 15-20 minutes. Roll out balls with a rolling pin until thin and round (7-8" diameter). Brown on a hot griddle until bubbly. Turn once and brown other side. Remove from heat and keep warm.

Makes approximately 1 dozen tortillas.

Whole Wheat Tortillas

1 tsp. SALT
1 tsp. BAKING POWDER
2 cups WHOLE WHEAT FLOUR
2 Tbsp. VEGETABLE OIL
1 cup (approx.) WARM WATER

In a medium size bowl, sift salt, baking powder and flour together. Add oil and mix well. Add water, a little at a time while working the mixture with your hands. Add only enough water to allow the dough to form a soft ball and no longer stick to the sides of the bowl. Knead the dough ball in the bowl or on a floured board. Divide dough to form separate balls the size of an egg. Using a floured board, roll out each ball with a rolling pin to the size of a salad or dinner plate. Cook on ungreased pancake griddle or skillet, turning until tortilla is lightly browned on both sides.

Makes 8-10 tortillas.

Tortillas Chiquitas

These tasty little tortillas are the perfect size for appetizers.

3 cups WHOLE WHEAT FLOUR   1/2 cup VEGETABLE OIL
1 tsp. SALT   1 cup WARM WATER
1/4 cup BUTTER

In a mixing bowl, sift flour and salt together. Blend butter and oil with flour mixture. When well blended, add warm water and mix. Place on a floured board and knead until dough is smooth. With a rolling pin, roll dough to 1/16 inch thickness. Using a biscuit cutter, cut dough into 2-3 inch round circles. Using just enough oil to grease bottom of skillet, brown tortilla until golden brown and bubbly, turn and brown other side. Keep warm if using or freeze.

Makes 20-24 tortillas.

Chocolate Tortillas

If you love chocolate, these are fun to make! Have plenty of mini-chocolate chips on hand and try to save some for the tortillas!

3 cups FLOUR
1/2 tsp. BAKING POWDER
1/2 tsp. SALT
1/4 cup SEMI-SWEETENED MINI-
    CHOCOLATE MORSELS
1/4 cup INSTANT COCOA POWDER
1 tsp. CINNAMON
1 Tbsp. VANILLA
1 cup WARM WATER
1/4 cup CORN OIL

Mix first six ingredients together in a bowl. Add vanilla and oil and blend. Slowly add 1 cup of warm water and mix well. Dough should be smooth and pliable. If dough is too dry, add more water and knead. Form into balls about the size of a small-medium egg. Rub each ball with oil and cover with towel. Let sit 15-20 minutes. Roll with a rolling pin until thin and well rounded. Lightly brown on a hot griddle until bubbly then turn once to brown the other side.

Makes approximately 1 dozen, 7-8" tortillas.

Note: Milk chocolate morsels can be substituted if desired.

Jalapeño Tortillas

These can be very hot! If you're not sure of your guest's tolerance omit the dried jalapeños.

3 cups FLOUR
1/2 tsp. BAKING POWDER
1/2 tsp. SALT
1 Tbsp. JALAPEÑO PEPPER, dried
1 Tbsp. BLACK PEPPER, crushed
1 Tbsp. GARLIC SALT
2 oz. JALAPEÑO PEPPERS, diced
1/4 cup CORN OIL
1 cup WARM WATER

Mix dry ingredients together in a bowl. Add diced jalapeño peppers and oil and blend. Slowly add warm water. Mix well. Dough should be smooth and pliable. If dough is too dry, add more water and knead dough. Make into balls about the size of a small-medium egg. Rub each ball with oil and cover with towel. Let sit 15-20 minutes. Roll with a rolling pin until thin and round (7-8" diameter). Lightly brown on a hot griddle until bubbly. Turn once and brown the other side.

Makes approximately 1 dozen tortillas.

Coconut Tortillas

3 cups FLOUR
1/2 tsp. BAKING POWDER
1/2 tsp. SALT
1 cup SHREDDED COCONUT
1/2 cup BROWN SUGAR
2 Tbsp. ALMOND FLAVORING
1/4 cup CORN OIL
1 cup WARM WATER

Mix first five ingredients together in a bowl. Fold almond flavoring and oil into dry mixture. Slowly add 1 cup of warm water and mix well. Dough should be smooth and pliable. If dough is too dry, add more water and knead dough. Form into balls about the size of a small-medium egg. Rub each ball with oil and cover with towel. Let sit 15-20 minutes. Roll with a rolling pin until thin and well rounded (7-8" diameter). Lightly brown on a hot griddle until bubbly then turn once to brown the other side.

Makes approximately 1 dozen tortillas.

Blue Corn Tortillas

2 cups WATER
1 tsp. SALT
2 cups BLUE CORNMEAL

In a saucepan, add salt and water and bring to a boil. Place blue cornmeal in a bowl and gradually add the boiling water, stirring constantly, until mixture becomes a firm dough. Cool for about 15 minutes. Divide the dough into 1 1/2" balls. Shape each ball into flat, thin, 6-inch tortillas by pressing, rolling, or patting with hands. Lightly brown on both sides in heated skillet.

Makes approximately 10-12 tortillas.

Blueberry Tortillas

3 cups FLOUR
1/2 tsp. BAKING POWDER
1/2 tsp. SALT
1 tsp. CINNAMON
3 Tbsp. SUGAR
2 Tbsp. VANILLA
1/4 cup CORN OIL
1 1/2 cup BLUEBERRIES, crushed or puréed
1/2-3/4 cup WARM WATER

Mix dry ingredients together in a bowl and stir. Fold vanilla and oil into mixture. Add blueberries and blend. Slowly add 1/2 cup of warm water. Mix well. Dough should be smooth and pliable. If dough is too dry, add more water and knead dough. Make into balls about the size of a small-medium egg. Rub each ball with oil and cover with towel. Let sit 15-20 minutes. Roll out balls with a rolling pin until thin and round (7-8" diameter). Lightly brown on a hot griddle until bubbly. Turn once and brown other side. Remove from heat and keep warm.

Makes 1 dozen tortillas.

May substitute **BLACKBERRIES, CRANBERRIES, RASP-BERRIES,** etc.

Cinnamon Tortillas

3 cups FLOUR
1/2 tsp. BAKING POWDER
1/2 tsp. SALT
2 tsp. CINNAMON
1 tsp. NUTMEG
4 Tbsp. SUGAR
2 Tbsp. VANILLA
1/4 cup CORN OIL
1 cup WARM WATER

Mix dry ingredients together in a bowl. Add vanilla and oil and blend. Slowly add 1 cup of warm water and mix well. Dough should be smooth and pliable. If dough is too dry, add more water and knead dough. Make into balls about the size of a small-medium egg. Rub each ball with oil and cover with towel. Let sit 15-20 minutes. Roll each ball flat and thin with a rolling pin to 7-8" diameter. Lightly brown on a hot griddle until bubbly. Turn once and brown the other side.

Makes approximately 1 dozen tortillas.

Tortilla Chips

Serve these chips when they're nice and hot!

CORN TORTILLAS
SALT

There are two methods for making tortilla chips— frying and baking. To fry them, first cut corn tortillas into either strips or triangles and fry in corn oil for about one minute on each side or until crispy. Take them out and drain on several paper towels. Salt to desired taste.

To bake the chips, cut tortillas into triangles, preheat oven to 450° and place the tortillas on a baking sheet for 4-5 minutes each side. Salt to desired taste.

Appetizers

Sombrero Roll-ups

*This makes a great appetizer for a southwestern meal. Bring these to a
pot luck party, and you'll always be invited back!*

4 (10-12") FLOUR TORTILLAS
1 pkg. (8 oz.) CREAM CHEESE
GROUND PEPPER
LETTUCE leaves
1 pkg. (4 oz.) BEAN SPROUTS
2 med. TOMATOES, diced
8-12 slices TURKEY
1 cup sliced BLACK OLIVES, drained
2 med. AVOCADOS, sliced

Place tortilla on flat surface. Spread cream cheese, generously
covering entire top of tortilla. Sprinkle tortilla with ground pepper to
taste. Arrange lettuce leaves to cover 2/3 of top, leaving the bottom
1/3 tortilla free of ingredients. Layer bean sprouts, tomatoes, turkey
slices, black olives, and avocados. Begin rolling tortilla from top to
bottom 1/3, applying medium pressure as you roll. Prepare remaining tortillas. Slice each tortilla into 6-8 pieces. Arrange on serving
dish. Garnish with lettuce leaves.

Guacamole Grande

1 can (4 oz.) GREEN CHILES, chopped
1 LIME, juiced
3 GREEN ONIONS, finely chopped
3 med. TOMATOES, chopped
GARLIC SALT, to taste
1 lg. AVOCADO, diced
TORTILLA CHIPS

Combine all ingredients except chips and mix well. Serve with
tortilla chips. Makes about 2 cups of guacamole.

Southwestern Jalapeño Bean Dip

If you want a hot and spicy dip, this is it! Be careful here, you might want to post a warning sign — Hot!

4 cups cooked PINTO BEANS, with juice
8 oz. VELVEETA® CHEESE
1/4 cup (1/2 stick) BUTTER or MARGARINE
3 JALAPEÑOS, stems removed
TORTILLA CHIPS

Using a food processor or blender, mix the cheese, butter or margarine and jalapeños. Blend until smooth and place in a bowl. Serve hot or cold with tortilla chips.

Rocky Point Shrimp Tortillas

1/2 cup CHEDDAR CHEESE, shredded
1 1/2 tsp. MAYONNAISE
1 can (4 oz.) small SHRIMP
1 clove GARLIC, minced
1/2 tsp. SALT
1 stick BUTTER or MARGARINE
8 (8") FLOUR TORTILLAS

In a food processor or blender, blend cheddar cheese, mayonnaise, and shrimp. Add garlic and salt. Fold in butter or margarine. Mix well. Spread on tortillas. Refrigerate until ready to serve. Remove from refrigerator and broil until hot and bubbly. Cut tortilla into four quarters and serve warm.

Note: May substitute crabmeat for shrimp.

Piña Quesadillas

1 can (8 oz.) DOLE® CRUSHED PINEAPPLE, well drained
1 sm. TOMATO, chopped
2 Tbsp. GREEN ONION, finely chopped
2 Tbsp. JALAPEÑO CHILES, chopped
1 cup (4 oz.) JACK CHEESE, shredded
4 (8") FLOUR TORTILLAS
VEGETABLE COOKING SPRAY
SOUR CREAM, optional

Combine drained pineapple, tomato, green onion and peppers in a small bowl. Sprinkle pineapple mixture and cheese evenly over one-half of each tortilla. Fold each tortilla in half to form quesadillas, lightly pressing down. Place two quesadillas in large skillet sprayed with vegetable cooking spray. Cook over medium heat three to five minutes or until cheese melts, turning once halfway through cooking. Remove from skillet and repeat cooking with remaining two quesadillas. Cut each quesadilla into three triangles. Serve with sour cream, if desired.

Hot Frijole Dip

1 can (15 oz.) REFRIED BEANS
1 can (16 oz.) TOMATOES, drained and chopped
1 can (4 oz.) GREEN CHILES, diced
1/4 cup ONION, diced
1/4 tsp. SALT
1/4 tsp. GARLIC SALT, optional
1 cup CHEDDAR or JACK CHEESE, shredded
TORTILLA CHIPS

Add refried beans to skillet. Combine tomatoes, chiles, onion and seasonings with the beans. Fold in cheese and stir. Heat until cheese melts, stirring occasionally. Serve warm with crispy tortilla chips. This dip makes a great filling for warmed tortillas, too.

Cold Frijole Dip

1 can (15 oz.) REFRIED BEANS
2 Tbsp. ONION, grated
1 tsp. CHILI POWDER
1 clove GARLIC, minced

1 tsp. SALT
1 sm. pkg. (3 oz.) CREAM
   CHEESE
TORTILLA CHIPS

Mix refried beans, onion, chili powder, garlic, and salt. Soften cream cheese (may substitute non-fat cream cheese). Add cream cheese to bean mixture and mix well. Refrigerate until ready to serve. Serve with tortilla chips and enjoy!

> *Use caution when using chili powder. Too much*
> *can leave a dish with a bitter taste.*

South-of-the-Border Guacamole Dip

This dip is so good you will be tempted to make it an entire meal.
Just add the margaritas!

2 med. RIPE AVOCADOS, halved
4 oz. NON-FAT CREAM CHEESE
2 tsp. LIME JUICE
1/4 tsp. TABASCO®
1/4 tsp. SALT
1/2 tsp. WORCESTERSHIRE SAUCE
TORTILLA CHIPS

Cut avocados in half, lengthwise, and remove pits. Scoop flesh from skin. Soften cream cheese and add to mashed avocados. Add remaining ingredients and blend until smooth. Serve with tortilla chips for a zesty dip.

Pinto Bean Dip

1 can (16 oz.) PINTO BEANS, drained
1/4 cup (1/2 stick) BUTTER or MARGARINE
1 clove GARLIC, minced
1/4 tsp. CUMIN SEED, crushed
1 cup (4 oz.) CHEDDAR CHEESE, shredded
TORTILLA CHIPS

Reserve liquid from beans after draining and set aside. Add butter or margarine to small skillet and melt. Add beans to melted butter, stir and mash. Cook for approximately 5 minutes on med-high heat. Blend in garlic and stir. Add cumin seed and continue stirring. Slowly add liquid from beans, one teaspoon at a time, until desired consistency for dipping. Add cheese and stir until cheese melts. Serve this dip warm with tortilla chips.

Chihuahua Cheese Crisp

1 (10-12") FLOUR TORTILLA
1 tsp. BUTTER, melted
2 cups (8 oz.) LONGHORN, JACK or CHEDDAR CHEESE
1/4 cup BLACK OLIVES, diced
1/4 cup ONIONS, diced
1 can (4 oz.) GREEN CHILES, diced

Place tortilla in oven under broiler just until warm to touch. Do not allow to get crisp. Spread the top lightly with melted butter. Generously sprinkle cheese over entire top of tortilla and top with remaining ingredients. Return to broiler and allow cheese to melt and bubble. Serve steaming hot for a delightful treat.

Quick Tortilla Bites

This neat little treat builds a big appetite for a big feast!

2 pkgs. (8 oz. each) CREAM CHEESE
1 cup PICANTE SAUCE
4 Tbsp. BLACK OLIVES, chopped
12 (10 ") FLOUR TORTILLAS

In a medium bowl, mix cream cheese, picante sauce and olives. Spread mixture over each flour tortilla. Roll up and chill for at least one hour. When ready to serve, slice each tortilla into 8 portions and secure with toothpicks.

Taco Dip

1 can (16 oz.) REFRIED BEANS	1 pkg. TACO SEASONING MIX
3 med. AVOCADOS	3 GREEN ONIONS, chopped
2 Tbsp. LEMON JUICE	3 TOMATOES, coarsely chopped
1 tsp. SALT	1/2 cup RIPE OLIVES, chopped
1/4 tsp. BLACK PEPPER	16 oz. CHEDDAR CHEESE,
1 cup SOUR CREAM	grated
1/4 cup SALAD DRESSING	TORTILLA CHIPS

On a large platter, evenly spread refried beans. Mash avocados in a separate bowl. Add lemon juice, salt and pepper. Mix well. Spread avocado mixture over refried beans. Next, combine sour cream, salad dressing and taco seasoning mix. Spread over refried bean mixture. Sprinkle bean mixture with onions, tomatoes and olives and top with cheddar cheese. Serve cold with tortilla chips.

Serves 10-12.

Charlie Brown's Mexican Roll-ups

1 pkg. (8 oz.) CREAM CHEESE, softened
1 pt. (16 oz.) SOUR CREAM
1 can (4 oz.) diced GREEN CHILES, drained
1/2 tsp. GARLIC POWDER
1 lb. LONGHORN CHEESE, grated
1 can (4 oz.) BLACK OLIVES, diced
12 (10-12") FLOUR TORTILLAS

Mix all ingredients together and chill. Spread mixture on tortillas. Begin to roll tortilla, starting with edge closest to you. When all tortillas are filled and rolled, cover and chill well before slicing. Slice each roll-up into 8 sections and secure with toothpicks. Serve with picante or taco sauce.

Tijuana Tortilla Treats

1 can (4 oz.) GREEN CHILES, diced
2 med. TOMATOES, diced
2 GREEN ONIONS, diced
1 sm. can (4 1/2 oz.) DEVILED HAM
1 can (4 oz.) BLACK OLIVES, diced
2 pkgs. (8 oz. each) CREAM CHEESE, softened
8 (10-12") FLOUR TORTILLAS

Mix together chiles, tomatoes, onions, meat and olives. Fold in softened cream cheese. Spread mixture over top of each tortilla. Roll tortilla into flute-like shape and chill for at least one-half hour. Slice each roll-up into 8 bite-size pieces and secure with toothpicks. Serve chilled.

For variation serve warm with your favorite salsa on the side.

Santa Fe Queso Dip

4 GREEN ONIONS, chopped
1 Tbsp. BUTTER or MARGARINE
1 can (4 oz.) GREEN CHILES, diced and drained
2 med. TOMATOES, chopped
1/4 cup BEER
BOTTLED HOT PEPPER SAUCE, to taste
1/4 tsp. SALT
1 1/2 cup JACK CHEESE, shredded
1 1/2 cup CHEDDAR CHEESE, shredded
TORTILLA CHIPS

Sauté onion in butter or margarine until transparent. When onion is tender, stir in chiles and tomato. Add beer, hot pepper sauce and salt. Simmer uncovered for approximately 5-10 minutes. Stir in cheeses, a little at a time, until melted. Serve immediately with tortilla chips for a zesty treat.

Keep in warming dish while serving. Add a small amount of warm beer if too thick.

Oaxaca Guacamole

2 lg. ripe AVOCADOS, peeled and pitted
1 med. TOMATO, peeled, seeded and chopped
1 GREEN ONION, chopped
2 NEW MEXICO GREEN CHILE PEPPERS, seeded and chopped
1/2 tsp. SALT
1/8 tsp. BLACK PEPPER, freshly ground
3 Tbsp. LEMON JUICE
TORTILLA CHIPS

Chop avocados coarsely. Place in large mixing bowl and mash until smooth. Add tomato, onion and chiles. Mix gently yet thoroughly. Add salt, pepper and lemon juice. Stir. Cover tightly with plastic wrap until ready to serve. Use as a dip with tortilla chips.

Nachos Supreme

*Nachos are a great treat for parties or whenever your favorite sports are on TV.
In fact, nachos are a great snack anytime!*

1/2 lb. CHORIZO or GROUND BEEF
TORTILLA CHIPS
1/2 cup CHEDDAR CHEESE, shredded
1/2 cup JACK CHEESE, shredded
1/2 cup GUACAMOLE DIP, of choice
1/2 cup SOUR CREAM
1/2 cup RIPE OLIVES, sliced
1/2 cup JALAPEÑO PEPPERS, diced

In a large skillet, break up chorizo (Mexican sausage) or ground beef. Cook until browned. Remove meat from pan and drain. Pat with paper towels to remove excess fat. Set aside. Next, spread tortilla chips to cover a large (12") oven-proof platter, allowing some overlap. Arrange meat evenly over tortilla chips. Sprinkle cheeses atop meat and chips. Bake chips in 350° oven for 5-7 minutes, or until cheese melts. Spoon favorite guacamole dip over cheese and meat, followed by sour cream. Top with olives and jalapeños. Serve warm.

Green Chile Cheese Nachos

TORTILLA CHIPS
1/2 cup CHEDDAR CHEESE, shredded
1/2 cup JACK CHEESE, shredded
1 can (4 oz.) GREEN CHILES, diced

Cover a large (12") oven-proof platter with tortilla chips. Sprinkle cheese atop chips. Bake chips in 350° oven for 5-7 minutes, or until cheese melts. Top with green chiles and serve.

Mexicali Bean Dip

2 cans (9 oz. ea.) BEAN DIP
1 cup (8 oz.) SOUR CREAM
1 pkg. (8 oz.) CREAM CHEESE
1 pkg. TACO SEASONING MIX
20 drops TABASCO®
1 cup GREEN ONIONS, diced
3 Tbsp. BLACK OLIVES, chopped
1/2 cup JACK or CHEDDAR CHEESE, shredded
TORTILLA CHIPS

In a medium mixing bowl, add all ingredients together with the exception of the cheese and chips. Blend with beater. Pour into ungreased glass baking dish. Sprinkle cheese on top to cover mixture. Bake in 350° oven until mixture is hot and cheese is melted. Serve warm with tortilla chips for a mouth-watering appetizer.

Crabmeat Pockets

8 oz. CRABMEAT
8 oz. CREAM CHEESE
1 tsp. GARLIC, granulated
1 EGG
SALT and WHITE PEPPER, to taste
2 Tbsp. OIL
TOOTHPICKS
12 (10-12") FLOUR TORTILLAS

Mix crabmeat, cream cheese, garlic and egg. Salt and pepper to taste. With a large-mouth glass, cut the tortillas into small circles. Place a small amount of the mixture in the center of each circle then fold in half. Sew each tortilla shut with toothpicks and fry in oil till brown and crisp.

Cooked pockets can be frozen and reheated in a 325° oven for 5-10 minutes. Serve with ranch dressing on a bed of lettuce leaves.

Nachos Arizona Style

1 lb. LEAN GROUND BEEF
SALT AND PEPPER, to taste
HOT SAUCE, use sparingly
1 lg. RED ONION, chopped
1 can (16 oz.) REFRIED BEANS
1 can (4 oz.) GREEN CHILES, chopped
2 cups LONGHORN CHEESE, shredded
1 cup JACK CHEESE, shredded
3/4 cup TACO SAUCE
1/4 cup GREEN ONIONS, chopped
1 cup RIPE BLACK OLIVES, pitted
1 cup SOUR CREAM
1 lg. RED BELL PEPPER, chopped

First cook the ground beef until brown, drain fat and season to taste. Add 2 to 3 drops of hot sauce and onion. Spread beans in a large 9 x 13 rectangular ovenproof dish and top with cooked meat. Sprinkle with green chiles, both cheeses and taco sauce. Bake for 20 to 25 minutes in a 400° oven.

Remove from oven and garnish with green onions, black olives, sour cream and bell pepper. Place tortilla chips around the edges of the dish and serve.

Serves 10-12.

Poco Crisps

8 (10-12") FLOUR TORTILLAS
8 oz. LONGHORN or CHEDDAR CHEESE, grated
1 cup sliced BLACK OLIVES, drained

Place tortilla on cutting surface. Cut a 2-3" circle from tortilla (use an inverted drinking glass as a guide.) Repeat process until you achieve desired number of circles. Cover tortilla circles with cheese. Garnish with black olives. Place on cookie sheet and broil until cheese melts. Serve hot.

Breakfasts

Rio Verde Breakfast Special

This is a great recipe for a Sunday morning. As you read your paper, the smell of the green chiles will fill the kitchen!

6 lg. EGGS
1/4 cup MILK
1/8 tsp. SALT
1 Tbsp. BUTTER or MARGARINE
1/2 cup JACK CHEESE, cubed
1/2 cup GREEN CHILES, seeded and diced
6 CORN TORTILLAS, softened
1/3 cup SOUR CREAM
1 ripe AVOCADO, peeled and sliced

In a mixing bowl, combine eggs, milk and salt and mix well. Melt butter or margarine in skillet. Add eggs to skillet and cook over medium heat, stirring gently. When eggs are almost set, add cheese and chiles. Cook until firm, or desired consistency. Fill each tortilla with egg mixture and fold. Top with sour cream and garnish with sliced avocado. Serve immediately.

Serves 6.

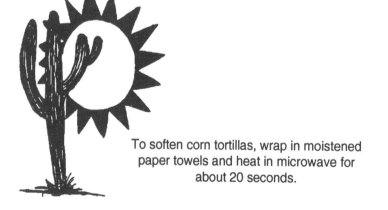

To soften corn tortillas, wrap in moistened paper towels and heat in microwave for about 20 seconds.

Apple Tortillas

1/3 cup BUTTER or MARGARINE
3 lbs. tart COOKING APPLES, peeled,
    cored and sliced
1/4 cup SUGAR
1 tsp. CINNAMON
8 (8") FLOUR TORTILLAS, softened
POWDERED SUGAR, as desired
WHIPPED CREAM, as desired

In a large skillet, melt butter or margarine over medium heat. Add sliced apples and stir. Blend in sugar and cinnamon and stir gently. Continue cooking apple mixture, stirring occasionally with a gentle hand. Remove from heat when apples begin to soften. Fill tortillas with apple mixture and fold in half. Serve hot, topped with powdered sugar and whipped cream. You can substitute canned apple pie filling, if desired in which case you would only have to heat the filling and place it in the tortillas.

For an evening dessert, top off apple tortillas with the following *Vanilla Sauce.*

Serves 6-8.

Vanilla Sauce

1 cup HEAVY CREAM
3 Tbsp. BRANDY
1 pt. VANILLA ICE CREAM, softened

Add cream to a mixing bowl and beat until thick. Add brandy and stir. Combine softened ice cream to cream and brandy mixture and stir. What a mouth-watering dessert!

Curried Breakfast Tortillas

*Try this recipe to **really** wake up your taste buds!*

1/4 cup BUTTER or MARGARINE
1/4 cup FLOUR
1/4 cup ONION, chopped
1 tsp. CURRY POWDER
2 1/2 cups MILK
SALT, to taste
PEPPER, to taste
6 HARD-COOKED EGGS, chopped

In a small saucepan, melt butter or margarine. Blend in flour and stir. Add onion and curry powder and cook over low heat for about 2 minutes. Gradually add milk to mixture, stirring continuously until sauce begins to thicken. Season with salt and pepper, as desired. Place chopped eggs in a mixing bowl and add just enough of the sauce to moisten eggs. Fill each softened tortilla with egg mixture, roll into flute-like shapes and place in greased baking dish. Pour remaining curried sauce over tortillas and heat under broiler until bubbly.

Serves 4.

You may substitute **BABY SHRIMP** or diced **CHICKEN** for the hard-cooked eggs for a dinner delight.

Chimayo Huevos Rancheros

This recipe was named Chimayo, after a small town in northern New Mexico, near Santa Fe.

2 slices BACON, diced
2 GREEN ONIONS, chopped
1 clove GARLIC, minced
1 can (4 oz.) GREEN CHILES, diced and drained
1 can (14 1/2 oz.) TOMATOES, chopped
8 EGGS
SALT, to taste
GROUND PEPPER, to taste
8 CORN TORTILLAS, softened
1 cup CHEDDAR CHEESE, shredded

In a large skillet, cook bacon until crisp. Remove from pan and drain on paper towels. Add onion, garlic, chiles and tomatoes to drippings and simmer for about 5 minutes on low heat. Break eggs into mixture and sprinkle with salt and pepper. Cover tightly and cook until eggs reach desired doneness. Using a spatula, remove eggs and place one in each tortilla. Spoon one tablespoon onion mixture over egg, top with a tablespoonful of cheese and fold. Add bacon to remaining onion mixture and pour over filled tortillas. Top with remaining cheese. Serve immediately.

Serves 8.

Jamón y Queso Quiche

(Ham and Cheese Quiche)

4 (8") FLOUR TORTILLAS
2 Tbsp. VEGETABLE OIL or VEGETABLE SPRAY
3 EGGS
1/3 cup MILK
1 Tbsp. FLOUR
1/2 cup HAM, diced
1 JALAPEÑO, peeled, seeded and diced
1 cup CHEDDAR CHEESE, grated
2 TOMATOES, chopped
SALT and PEPPER, to taste

Preheat oven to 400°. Lightly brush both sides of tortillas with oil (or spray lightly with vegetable spray). Press into custard cups or large muffin tins. Bake in oven until tortillas begin to turn golden brown. Remove and cool slightly. Beat eggs in medium bowl. Add milk, flour, ham, jalapeño, cheese and tomatoes. Stir until well mixed. Season to taste. Pour mixture into prebaked tortilla shells and bake at 400° for 20 minutes, or until set. Garnish plate with fruit and salsa and serve.

Serves 4.

Old Mexico Tortillas de Maíz

These tortillas have the taste of Old Mexico. They use whole corn kernels, canned, or taken right off the cob!

1 cup CORN KERNELS
1/3 cup VEGETABLE OIL

Tortilla batter:
  8 EGGS
  2 Tbsp. FLOUR
  1 1/2 tsp. SALT
  1/2 tsp. PEPPER, freshly ground

4 Tbsp. BUTTER
1/2 cup SOUR CREAM
2 Tbsp. fresh PARSLEY, finely chopped

Dry corn kernels by patting with a paper towel, if necessary. In a large skillet, heat oil on medium heat until it becomes cloudy. Add corn to oil and stir frequently for approximately 10 minutes, or until corn is golden brown. Using a slotted spoon, remove corn and place on a double layer of paper towels to drain. Set aside.

In a large bowl beat eggs until foamy. Blend in flour, salt and pepper. In a 6" skillet, melt a tablespoon of butter over medium heat. Pour 1/4 of egg mixture into skillet. Sprinkle with 2 tablespoons of corn when edges of tortilla begin to set. Next, take a spatula and push the edges toward the center. Tilt pan until the uncooked batter moves to edges. Cover complete surface with batter. Continue cooking until entire batter is set and bottom of tortilla is golden brown. Turn tortilla over with spatula and cook approximately 1 minute longer until flipped side is browned. Transfer cooked tortilla to warmed platter. Stir batter and repeat process until all batter is used. Serve each tortilla topped with a tablespoon of sour cream and a pinch of parsley.

Serves 4.

Tortillas por Desayuno

(Tortillas for Breakfast)

8 oz. CHORIZO SAUSAGE
1 pkg. (16 oz.) frozen HASH BROWN POTATOES
2 GREEN BELL PEPPER, chopped
1 RED BELL PEPPER, chopped
1 med. ONION, chopped
6 EGGS, beaten
1 cup CHEDDAR CHEESE, grated
4 FLOUR TORTILLAS
1 cup PICANTE SAUCE, optional

Brown sausage in frying pan; drain on paper towels and crumble. Add hash browns, peppers and onion to frying pan and sauté until onion is golden. Remove to a bowl and add chorizo. Lower heat to medium, add small amount of oil if necessary, and pour in eggs. Scramble until just moist. To serve, place a large scoop of potato mixture on a warmed tortilla, top with eggs and cheese. Add picante sauce if desired, roll up and enjoy.

Serves 4.

Soups & Salads

Enchilada Soup

Enchilada soup is a wonderful Mexican-style home remedy for a cold.

4 cups BEEF STOCK
2 ONIONS, diced
2 CELERY STALKS, diced
2 cloves GARLIC
4 Tbsp. CHILI POWDER
1/2 cup FLOUR
1/4 cup VEGETABLE OIL
1 can (4 oz.) SLICED OLIVES
3 TOMATOES, diced
SALT and PEPPER, to taste

Garnish:
   CHEDDAR CHEESE, grated
   JACK CHEESE, grated
   CORN TORTILLA STRIPS

Boil beef stock with onions, celery and garlic until onions are soft. In a bowl, mix chili powder, flour and oil. Next, slowly add chili mixture to stock while mixing the stock briskly with a whisk. Mix until the stock reaches the consistency of a thin stew. Add olives and diced tomatoes to soup mixture. Salt and pepper to taste.

Serve in individual bowls garnished with tortilla strips, jack and cheddar cheese.

Serves 8.

Sopa de Pollo Verde

Green chiles and chicken blend together here for a great soup.

1 lb. CHICKEN
4 cups CHICKEN STOCK
4 CELERY STALKS, sliced
1 ONION, sliced
1 Tbsp. FRESH GARLIC, chopped
1 cup GREEN CHILES, diced
1 tsp. CUMIN

1/2 tsp. CORIANDER
1/2 tsp. OREGANO
1 cup WATER
2/3 cup CORNSTARCH
SALT and PEPPER, to taste
TORTILLA STRIPS

Remove fat and skin from chicken. Add chicken to chicken stock and boil. Add the next seven ingredients to stock. Cook until chicken is done and onions and celery are soft. In a small bowl, combine water and cornstarch and stir until blended. Add cornstarch mixture to soup and stir until it reaches desired consistency. Salt and pepper to taste. Garnish with tortilla strips.

Serves 8.

Mexican Chicken Soup

2 cups GREEN CHILES, chopped
1 cup COOKED CHICKEN, chopped
1/2 cup ONION, chopped
1 tsp. GARLIC SALT
1 sm. TOMATO, peeled and chopped

1 tsp. KOSHER SALT
1 1/2 cups CHICKEN BROTH
1 1/2 cups HALF AND HALF
TORTILLA STRIPS

Combine chiles, chicken, onion, tomato, garlic and kosher salts in chicken broth. Bring to a boil, reduce heat and simmer for 45 minutes. If mixture is too thick, add more broth. (No more than one additional cup.) When ready to serve, add half and half and tortilla strips. Warm to a boil and serve immediately.

Serves 4.

Tortillas con Sopa de Carne

(Tortillas and Meat Soup)

1 lb. BEEF, cubed (chuck, sirloin, or stew meat)
2 tsp. VEGETABLE OIL
1 lg. ONION, sliced
4 CELERY STALKS, sliced
3 CARROTS, peeled and sliced
1 Tbsp. FRESH GARLIC, chopped
1 tsp. OREGANO
1 tsp. CUMIN
1 tsp. PARSLEY
4 cups BEEF BROTH
1/2 tsp. SALT
1/2 tsp. BLACK PEPPER
TORTILLA STRIPS OR CHIPS

Brown meat in oil. Add onions, celery and carrots to browned meat. Cook until onions are soft. Add garlic, oregano, cumin, parsley and sauté briefly. Add beef stock, bring to a boil and simmer until carrots are semi-soft. Salt and pepper to taste. This soup can be frozen and reheated for a quick tasty meal!

Garnish with tortilla strips or chips.

Serves 8.

Green Chile Soup

1 ONION, diced
4 CELERY STALKS, diced
1 Tbsp. GARLIC, minced
2 tsp. VEGETABLE OIL
4 cups CHICKEN STOCK

2 cups GREEN CHILES, diced
1 tsp. CUMIN
1/4 cup WATER
3 Tbsp. CORNSTARCH
TORTILLA STRIPS

Sauté onions, celery and garlic in oil until onions are soft. Add chicken stock, bring to a boil then reduce heat to simmer. Add green chiles and cumin. In a separate bowl, mix water and cornstarch until blended. Add cornstarch mixture to soup to thicken. Salt and pepper to taste. Garnish with tortilla strips.

Serves 8.

Blue Corn Salad

1 cup BLUE CORN TORTILLA CHIPS, crushed
1 pkg. (8 oz.) FROZEN PETITE PEAS, thawed
4 Tbsp. BACON BITS
1 cup BEAN SPROUTS
6 GREEN ONIONS
1/2 lb. FRESH MUSHROOMS
3 hard-boiled EGGS
4 BABY CARROTS, sliced
1/2 cup PARMESAN CHEESE
2 Tbsp. GREEN CHILES, diced
1/2 head ICEBERG LETTUCE
1/2 cup MAYONNAISE
2 Tbsp. SUGAR

Mix all ingredients together in a large brightly colored bowl and chill for 2 hours. Serve with salsa on the side.

Serves 6.

South-of-the-Border Sizzling Chicken Salad

2 cups cooked CHICKEN, diced
2 cups CELERY, finely chopped
1/2 cup ALMONDS, slivered
1/4 tsp. SALT
2 Tbsp. ONION, grated
2 Tbsp. LEMON JUICE
1 cup (or less) MAYONNAISE
1/2 cup CHEDDAR CHEESE, grated
1 cup TORTILLA CHIPS, crushed

Combine all ingredients except cheese and tortilla chips. Place chicken mixture in a 1 1/2-2 quart casserole dish. Combine cheese and tortilla chips and sprinkle evenly over chicken mixture. Bake in pre-heated 350° oven for 10 minutes or until heated through.

Serves 4.

Chef's Salad—Mexican-Style

1 lb. GROUND BEEF
1/2 cup KIDNEY BEANS, drained
1 lg. RIPE AVOCADO
1 head ICEBERG LETTUCE
4 med. TOMATOES, diced

1 ONION, chopped
1 cup JACK CHEESE, shredded
1 cup SALAD DRESSING
TORTILLA CHIPS, crushed
SALSA, optional

In a medium skillet, sauté ground beef until brown. Drain. Add beans to beef and simmer for approximately 10 minutes. Drain and allow to cool. Chop avocado, reserving a few slices for garnish. Tear lettuce and place in a bowl. Toss remaining ingredients and the beef mixture with lettuce. Place in salad bowls. Garnish with avocado slices and top with crushed tortilla chips.

Serves 8.

Mexican Camarón Salad

(Mexican Shrimp Salad)

1 head LETTUCE
8-12 med. SHRIMP, cooked and deveined
1 ripe AVOCADO, diced
1 cup GREEN ONION, chopped
4 Tbsp. ROMANO CHEESE
1 cup PEAS
8 Tbsp. VINEGAR
4 Tbsp. OIL
4 CORN TORTILLAS
1 cup REFRIED BEANS, heated
1 cup CHEDDAR CHEESE, shredded

Wash and drain lettuce. Tear lettuce and place in a large salad bowl. Add shrimp, avocado, onion, Romano cheese and peas. Add vinegar and oil to lettuce mixture and toss. Set aside. Place each tortilla between two wet paper towels. Heat in microwave on high for 1 minute. Remove and transfer to individual dishes. Layer each tortilla with 1/4 cup of hot refried beans followed by 1/4 cup cheddar cheese. Top each tortilla with a generous amount of lettuce mixture and serve.

Serves 4.

Arizona Taco Salad

1 lb. LEAN GROUND BEEF
1 envelope TACO SEASONING
1/4 cup WATER
1 med. ONION, diced
1 Tbsp. CHILI POWDER
1 tsp. GARLIC SALT
1 can (16 oz.) KIDNEY BEANS
3 cups ICEBERG LETTUCE, shredded
1/2 cup CHEDDAR CHEESE, grated
6 CHERRY TOMATOES,
    sliced in half
1/2 cup BLACK OLIVES
Lowfat SOUR CREAM
SALSA
TORTILLA CHIPS, mixture of colors

Brown and drain ground beef and add taco seasoning, water, onion, chili powder, salt and kidney beans. Simmer for 15 minutes. Combine the lettuce, cheese, tomatoes and olives in large bowl. Divide lettuce mixture between individual salad bowls and pour the beef mixture over each. Garnish each serving with sour cream and salsa. Add colored tortilla chips around the edge of each bowl.

Serves 4.

Spanish Cottage Cheese

1 pint SMALL CURD COTTAGE CHEESE
2 oz. GREEN CHILES, diced
1 sm. TOMATO, chopped
1 Tbsp. PIMENTOS, chopped

Combine all ingredients and chill for 2-3 hours. Serve with tortilla chips for a spicy variety salad.

Yields about 2 cups.

Main Dishes

Bean Enchiladas

An innovative approach to a meatless enchilada.

1 can (16 oz.) REFRIED BEANS
2 cups JACK CHEESE, shredded
1 can (4 oz.) GREEN CHILES, chopped
1 can (19 oz.) ENCHILADA SAUCE
10-12 CORN TORTILLAS

In a medium bowl, combine beans, 1 cup of cheese and green chiles. Set aside. Add enchilada sauce to a medium skillet and bring to a boil. Remove from heat and dip a tortilla in to soften. Spoon in approximately three tablespoons of bean mixture down the center of each tortilla and roll. Place tortillas in a 13 x 9 inch baking dish seam side down. Pour remaining enchilada sauce on top of enchiladas. Sprinkle top with remaining cup of cheese. Bake at 350° for approximately 20-25 minutes. Serve piping hot. Garnish with guacamole and sour cream.

Serves 6.

Mexican Turkey Enchiladas

A creative use for turkey, these enchiladas provide
a delicious southwestern meal.

1 lb. GROUND TURKEY
1 1/4 cups SALSA
1 can (15 oz.) BLACK BEANS, drained
1 can (7 oz.) GREEN CHILES, diced and drained
1 cup SOUR CREAM
1/2 cup CHEDDAR CHEESE, shredded
1 Tbsp. FLOUR
3 (10-12") FLOUR TORTILLAS
1 cup LETTUCE, shredded
1/2 cup TOMATOES, chopped

Sauté ground turkey in a large saucepan until brown. Remove from heat and drain well, if necessary. Add 1 cup salsa to turkey and stir well. Add beans to mixture and set aside. Mix together chiles, sour cream, 1/4 cup of cheddar cheese and flour. Place one tortilla in bottom of 10" round, non-stick ceramic or glass oven-proof dish. Add 3/4 cup of turkey mixture and 1/2 of sour cream mixture. Top with second tortilla. Follow with 3/4 cup of turkey mixture and remaining sour cream mixture. Top with tortilla and balance of turkey mixture. Bake in a pre-heated 350° oven for 25 minutes or until heated. Allow to stand 5 minutes. Garnish with lettuce, tomatoes, balance of salsa and cheddar cheese. Cut into wedges and serve.

Serves 4.

Southwestern
Enchilada Stack

*This dish is similar to lasagna, with each layer serving up something
even more delicious.*

1/2 lb. GROUND BEEF
1 can (15 oz.) REFRIED BEANS
1 can (10 oz.) ENCHILADA SAUCE
1/2 cup BLACK OLIVES, chopped
5-6 CORN TORTILLAS
2 cups CHEDDAR CHEESE, shredded
1 cup ONION, diced
2 cloves GARLIC, minced
VEGETABLE COOKING SPRAY
LETTUCE, shredded
1/2 cup TOMATO, diced

Sauté ground beef in large skillet. Add garlic and onion and cook
until onion is translucent and beef is brown. Remove from heat and
drain well, if necessary. Return to stove. Stir in beans, enchilada
sauce, and olives. Simmer mixture approximately 15 minutes,
stirring occasionally. Place a tortilla in the bottom of a 9" baking dish
(non-stick or sprayed with vegetable cooking spray). Add beef
mixture and top with cheese. Repeat layering process until all
tortillas and meat mixture are used. Top with cheese and bake in pre-
heated 350° oven for 30 minutes. Garnish serving plates with
shredded lettuce and top with diced tomatoes. Serve with **salsa** and
sour cream, if desired.

Serves 4.

Chicken Enchiladas

4 CHICKEN BREASTS, boneless and skinned
WATER to cover
1/4 tsp. SALT
2 cups CHEDDAR CHEESE, shredded
2 cups MOZZARELLA CHEESE, shredded
1 sm. ONION, finely chopped
1/3 cup MILK
1 can (10 3/4 oz.) CREAM OF CHICKEN SOUP
1 can (10 3/4 oz.) CREAM OF CELERY SOUP
2 Tbsp. BUTTER
1 can (7 oz.) GREEN CHILES, diced and drained
1 sm. JALAPEÑO, peeled, seeded and diced
8-12 CORN TORTILLAS
1/2 cup VEGETABLE OIL

Put chicken breasts, salt and enough water to cover in a large soup kettle and bring to boil. Cook for 45 minutes on med-low heat. In a large bowl, combine cheeses and onion. Set aside. Remove chicken when done, retaining 3 cups of stock. Using a fork, shred chicken into thin, long pieces. Return shredded chicken to remaining stock in soup kettle and simmer. Add milk, chicken and celery soups, butter, chiles and jalapeño to shredded chicken and stir. Simmer approximately 10 minutes.

Meanwhile, soften tortillas by dipping each one into hot vegetable oil for a few seconds per side. Drain on paper towels. Prepare enchiladas by filling each tortilla with a portion of the chicken and cheese mixture. Roll and place seam side down in a baking dish. Top with remaining chicken mixture. Sprinkle cheese mixture on top. Bake in a 300° oven for approximately 15 minutes. Remove sizzling enchiladas and serve.

Serves 6-8.

Sante Fe Enchiladas

*Sante Fe, New Mexico has maintained a small town charm
and atmosphere for many years.*

1 lb. GROUND CHICKEN
2 cans (10 3/4 oz. each) CREAM OF MUSHROOM SOUP
1 cup CHEDDAR CHEESE, shredded
1 cup JACK CHEESE, shredded
2/3 cup MILK
1 med. NEW MEXICO CHILE, seeded and diced
12 CORN TORTILLAS
1/2 cup VEGETABLE OIL

Sauté ground chicken in skillet until brown. Remove from heat and drain. In another saucepan, combine soup and 1/2 cup of cheddar and 1/2 cup jack cheese. Heat on medium until cheeses are melted. Add milk and continue to stir while mixture simmers for 5 minutes. Stir in the chile and cover. Let simmer for an additional 10 minutes. Add ground chicken to mixture.

Meanwhile, soften tortillas by dipping each one into hot vegetable oil for a few seconds per side. Drain on paper towels. Do not let tortillas get hard or brown.

Add just enough of the chicken mixture to cover the bottom of a shallow baking dish. Place a layer of corn tortillas over the mixture. Add another portion of the chicken mixture to cover the tortillas. Sprinkle with cheese. Repeat this layering process until all ingredients are used. Top with cheese. Bake at 350° until cheese bubbles.

Serves 6.

Tortillas Atún

(Tuna Tortillas)

What a great combination . . . a southwestern version of the tuna melt!

1 can (10 3/4 oz.) CREAM OF MUSHROOM SOUP
1 cup MILK
1 pkg. FROZEN BROCCOLI SPEARS, thawed and drained
1 can (10 oz.) TUNA FISH, drained and flaked
1 cup CHEDDAR CHEESE, shredded
1 can (2.8 oz.) FRENCH FRIED ONIONS
6 (8") FLOUR TORTILLAS
1 med. TOMATO, chopped

Place soup and milk in bowl and stir. Let stand while preparing other ingredients. Cut broccoli into 1-inch pieces. In a separate bowl, add broccoli, tuna, 1/2 cup of cheddar cheese, and 1/2 can of french fried onions. Stir in 3/4 cup of soup mixture.

Soften tortillas by dipping each one into hot vegetable oil for a few seconds per side. Drain on paper towels. Prepare enchiladas by adding equal amounts of tuna mixture to each tortilla. Roll each tortilla and place seam side down in lightly greased 9 x 13 baking dish. Stir tomatoes into remaining soup mixture and pour over the top of the enchiladas. Bake covered in 350° oven for 35 minutes. Top with remaining cheese and onions and bake, uncovered, for 5 minutes longer or until cheese bubbles.

Serves 4-6.

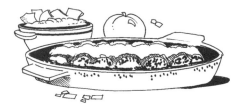

Tex-Mex Beef Tacos

Be sure to fill each taco to the top, then add a little more...now you have
a true Texas-style taco!

1 lb. GROUND BEEF
1 med. ONION, diced
2 cloves GARLIC, minced
1 Tbsp. CHILI POWDER
1 can (10 3/4 oz.) condensed TOMATO SOUP
8 TACO SHELLS, packaged
1 cup LETTUCE, shredded
2 med. TOMATOES, chopped
1 cup CHEDDAR CHEESE, shredded
2 med. AVOCADOS, chopped

In large saucepan, cook ground beef until it begins to brown. Stir in onion, garlic and chili powder. Continue cooking until meat is brown and onion is tender. Add soup and stir occasionally until mixture simmers. Remove from heat.

Fill each taco shell 1/2 full of meat mixture. Add lettuce and tomato. Sprinkle cheddar cheese over all. Top with avocado.

Serves 4.

Sour Cream Enchiladas

2 cans (10 3/4 oz. each) CREAM OF MUSHROOM SOUP
2 containers (16 oz. each) SOUR CREAM
1/3 cup MILK
2 doz. CORN TORTILLAS
2 cans (7 oz. each) GREEN CHILES, diced
2 bunches GREEN ONIONS, chopped
2 cups CHEDDAR or JACK CHEESE, shredded

In a large saucepan, mix together soup, sour cream and milk. Stir ingredients over medium heat until mixture boils. Remove from heat.

Soften tortillas by dipping each one into hot vegetable oil for a few seconds per side. Drain on paper towels. Do not let tortillas get hard or brown.

Place a small portion of the soup mixture in the bottom of a large baking dish. Put a layer of tortillas on top of mixture. Add another portion of soup mixture. Add green chiles, green onions and cheese. Continue to alternate tortillas, soup mixture, chiles, green onions and cheese layers until all ingredients are used. Top with soup mixture. Bake in pre-heated 350° oven for approximately 10-15 minutes or until enchiladas begin to bubble.

Serves 6-8.

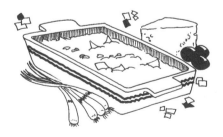

Saucy Southwestern Burros

1 lb. GROUND BEEF
1 can (16 oz.) TOMATOES, diced
1 tsp. DRY MUSTARD
1 tsp. CHILI POWDER
1 tsp. WORCESTERSHIRE SAUCE
1 clove GARLIC, minced
4 (10-12") FLOUR TORTILLAS
LETTUCE, shredded
2 lg. TOMATOES, chopped
1/2 cup CHEDDAR CHEESE, shredded

Sauté ground beef in skillet until brown. Drain, if necessary. Stir in undrained canned tomatoes, dry mustard, chili powder, Worcestershire sauce and garlic. Continue cooking until mixture begins to boil. Reduce heat and simmer uncovered for 15-20 minutes or until mixture thickens. Place meat mixture in center of tortilla, add lettuce and tomato. Top with cheese and fold burrito style.

Serves 4.

Pollo y Tortilla Chips
(Chicken and Tortilla Chips)

2 cups TORTILLA CHIPS, crushed
1/4 tsp. GARLIC SALT
1/8 tsp. PEPPER, freshly ground

1/4 tsp. OREGANO
1/8 tsp. PAPRIKA
2 1/2-3 lbs. CHICKEN

Place crushed tortilla chips, garlic salt, pepper, oregano and paprika in a large plastic bag. Shake well and set aside. Cut chicken into serving size pieces and rinse thoroughly in warm water. Coat moistened chicken by placing pieces, one at a time, in the tortilla mixture bag and shaking well until the entire chicken piece is covered. Place chicken, skin side up, in a lightly greased 9 x 13 baking dish. Bake in 375° oven for 60 minutes or until tender.

Serves 4.

Black Olive & Almond Beef Enchiladas

If you're looking for a unique taste, this is it!

2 cups cooked BEEF, shredded
1 cup BLACK OLIVES, chopped
1/4 cup BLANCHED ALMONDS, chopped
2 sm. ONIONS, diced
SALT, to taste
1 tsp. VEGETABLE OIL
3 cans (8 oz. each) TOMATO SAUCE
3 tsp. CHILI POWDER
1 can (7 oz.) GREEN CHILES, diced
12 (10-12") FLOUR TORTILLAS
1 cup JACK CHEESE, shredded
1/4 cup GREEN ONION, chopped

Mix beef, olives, almonds and half of onions. Salt to taste. Set aside. Add oil to skillet and sauté remaining onions until translucent. Add tomato sauce, chili powder and chiles to saucepan and simmer for approximately 10 minutes. Heat tortillas separately in sauce until softened. Remove each tortilla from sauce and place a portion of the beef mixture in center and roll. Arrange rolled tortillas, seam side down, in non-stick baking dish. Pour the remaining sauce over the top and sprinkle with 1/2 cup cheese. Bake at 350° for 15 minutes. Serve with balance of cheese and chopped green onions.

Serves 6-8.

Burros de Lengua
(Tongue Burros)

3-4 lb. BEEF TONGUE
2 cloves GARLIC
1/4 tsp. SALT
1 ONION, chopped
1 Tbsp. VEGETABLE OIL
1 can (4 oz.) GREEN CHILES, chopped
1 clove GARLIC, minced
2 cups TOMATOES, chopped
SALT, to taste
PEPPER, to taste
6-8 (10") FLOUR TORTILLAS

In large pot, cover beef tongue with water. Add 2 cloves of garlic and 1/4 tsp. salt. Cover tightly and boil until tongue is tender (approximately 3 hours).

While tongue is cooking, sauté onion with oil in small saucepan until transparent. Add chiles and simmer for 3-5 minutes. Add minced garlic and tomatoes. Continue to simmer mixture for an additional 5-10 minutes. Add salt and pepper to taste. Cover and chill until ready to use.

Remove tongue from pot when tender and dip in cold water. Slit outer skin and remove meat from outer shell. Peel and dice.

Add 2 cups diced, cooked beef tongue to large saucepan. Add onion mixture and simmer for approximately 3-5 minutes. Fill tortillas, fold and serve.

Serves 6-8.

Green Chile con Carne Burros

1 lb. STEWING BEEF, cubed
FLOUR
1 Tbsp. VEGETABLE OIL
2 lbs. GREEN CHILES
2-3 cloves GARLIC, diced
1/2 tsp. SALT
4 cups WATER or BEEF BROTH
6-8 (10-12") FLOUR TORTILLAS

Flour meat and brown in oil in a large skillet. Cut chiles in half, remove seeds and dice (if a hot mixture is desired, do not remove the seeds from the chiles). Add chiles and garlic to meat mixture. Stir in salt, water (or broth) and simmer for 1 hour or until meat is tender. Fill warmed tortillas with meat mixture and fold burrito style. Keep warm until ready to serve.

Serves 6.

Southwestern Wrap

It's a veggie burro! Delicious, nutritious, and a great light lunch.

1 Tbsp. CREAM CHEESE
1 (10-12") FLOUR TORTILLA
1/2 cup CUCUMBER, diced
1/8 cup TOFU, cubed
1/8 cup BLACK BEANS
1/4 cup CHEDDAR CHEESE, shredded
BEAN SPROUTS, optional
SALSA

Spread cream cheese to cover top surface of tortilla. Add cucumber, tofu and black beans to center of tortilla. Top with cheese followed by bean sprouts, if desired. Fold and serve warm or cold with salsa.

Serves 1.

Enchiladas con Chorizo y Queso

(Enchiladas with Sausage and Cheese)

1 lb. CHORIZO
1 lg. ONION, chopped
8-12 WHOLE WHEAT TORTILLAS, warmed
1 can (15 oz.) ENCHILADA SAUCE
2 cups JACK or CHEDDAR CHEESE, shredded
1 cup SOUR CREAM or YOGURT, optional

Remove chorizo casing, if necessary. Crumble chorizo into a skillet and sauté. Add onion and continue cooking until meat is done and onion is translucent. Drain, if necessary. Dip one tortilla at a time into enchilada sauce and place on platter. Add a layer of chorizo mixture and top with cheese. Repeat layering process until desired amount of tortillas and remaining chorizo and cheese are used. Heat enchilada sauce to a boil and pour over enchiladas. Top with sour cream or yogurt.

Serves 6-8.

Chicken & Avocado Tacos

2 ripe AVOCADOS, peeled and diced
1/2 cup MAYONNAISE
2 Tbsp. LEMON JUICE
1/4 tsp. TABASCO®
SALT, to taste
4-6 TACO SHELLS
1 cup CHICKEN, cooked and cubed
LETTUCE, shredded
4-6 RADISH roses

In a blender, mix avocado, mayonnaise, lemon juice, Tabasco and salt to taste. Partially fill taco shells with avocado mixture. Add chicken and top with shredded lettuce. Garnish each taco with a radish rose and serve.

Serves 4.

El Pollo del Rey
(The King's Chicken)

It is rumored that this dish was prepared for royalty in ancient times.
Now you can enjoy this regal recipe in your own castle!

1 can (4 oz.) MUSHROOMS, sliced and drained
1 Tbsp. BUTTER or MARGARINE
1/2 GREEN BELL PEPPER, chopped
1/2 cup ONION, chopped
2 CELERY STALKS, chopped
2 Tbsp. WHOLE WHEAT FLOUR
1/4 tsp. SALT
1/2 tsp. PEPPER, freshly ground
1/8 tsp. PAPRIKA
1/4 cup CHICKEN BROTH
1 cup MILK
1/4 cup HALF AND HALF
2 cups CHICKEN, cooked and diced
1 jar (4 oz.) PIMENTOS
4 (10-12") FLOUR TORTILLAS

Lightly sauté mushrooms in a medium size saucepan in melted butter. Add green pepper, onions and celery. Continue to sauté until onions become translucent. Stir in flour, salt, pepper and paprika and stir. While stirring, slowly add broth, milk and cream to saucepan. Cook mixture over medium heat, stirring frequently. Combine chicken and pimentos with mixture. Cook on low until completely heated. Soften and warm tortillas. Fill each tortilla with a generous portion of chicken mixture. Wrap and serve.

Serves 4.

Enchiladas Ternera
(Veal Enchiladas)

1/2 cup GREEN BELL PEPPER, chopped
1 lg. ONION, diced
1 Tbsp. VEGETABLE OIL
1 can (10 oz.) TOMATO PURÉE
2 tsp. CHILI POWDER
3 cups VEAL, cooked and cubed
1 cup BLACK OLIVES, diced
1/2 cup GREEN ONIONS, chopped
1/8 tsp. SALT
12 CORN TORTILLAS
2 cups ENCHILADA SAUCE
1/2 cup CHEDDAR CHEESE, shredded
1/2 cup JACK CHEESE, shredded
1 cup SOUR CREAM or YOGURT

In a medium size saucepan, sauté green peppers and onion in oil until onion becomes translucent. Add tomato purée and chili powder and cook on med-low until well blended. Keep purée mixture warm. Next, combine veal, olives, green onions, and salt. Mix well and set aside. Place a tortilla, one at a time, in the purée mixture until well saturated and warm. Remove, add a generous amount of meat mixture on top of tortilla and roll. Arrange in a large baking dish with seam side down. Repeat until all 12 tortillas are filled. Pour remaining sauce over top of enchiladas and sprinkle with cheese. Heat in 350° oven twenty or thirty minutes or until enchiladas are well heated and cheese is melted. Top with green onions and sour cream or yogurt.

Serves 6-8.

San Antonio Green Chile Burros

*San Antonio, Texas—the home of the very picturesque Riverwalk with its
sidewalk cafes. This recipe typifies the wonderful border cuisine.*

3-4 cups WATER
1/4 tsp.SALT
1/4 tsp. PEPPER
1/2 tsp. CHILI POWDER
1/4 tsp. GARLIC POWDER
1/4 tsp. ONION POWDER
1 (3-4 lb.) BEEF ROAST
3 med. TOMATOES, diced
1 can (4 oz.) GREEN CHILES, diced
3 Tbsp. CORNSTARCH
12 (10-12") FLOUR TORTILLAS, warmed

Place water in large pot. Combine salt, pepper, chili powder,
garlic powder, onion powder and add to water. Add beef roast and
cook for 3-4 hours, or until meat is tender. Remove roast from water
and shred. When meat is shredded, return to broth and add
tomatoes and chiles. Simmer for 30 minutes. Combine cornstarch
with 1/2 cup water until smooth and add to meat mixture stirring until
thickened. Add more water if necessary. Set aside. Fill warmed
tortillas with meat mixture and roll. Place on serving platter with seam
side down. Garnish with lettuce and tomato and serve salsa on the
side.

Serves 6-8.

Sandi's Chicken Burritos Enchilada Style

1 1/2 lbs. CHICKEN, cooked and shredded
CHILI POWDER, to taste
1 can (16 oz.) REFRIED BEANS, regular or non-fat
1 cup JACK CHEESE, shredded
1/2 cup GREEN ONIONS, chopped
1/2 cup BLACK OLIVES, chopped
1 can (4 oz.) GREEN CHILES, chopped
10 (12") FLOUR TORTILLAS
RED CHILE SAUCE (see recipe below)

Generously season chicken with chili powder. In a large saucepan cover chicken with water, bring to a boil and simmer with the lid on for 20-30 minutes, or until meat falls easily from bones. Cool and shred. Combine refried beans, 1/2 cup of cheese, onions, olives, and green chiles with shredded chicken. Spread mixture on each tortilla and roll into burrito shape. Place in baking dish coated with red sauce. Pour **Red Chile Sauce** (below) over burritos. Top with remaining 1/2 cup cheese. Bake in preheated, 350° oven for 30 minutes.

Serves 6-8.

Red Chile Sauce

8 WHOLE CHILE PEPPERS, dried
12 cups WATER
1/2 tsp. CUMIN
1/2 can (10 3/4 oz.) CREAM OF CHICKEN SOUP, undiluted
2 cans (4 oz. each) GREEN CHILES, chopped

Place peppers in saucepan with water and cumin. Bring to a boil, then reduce heat and simmer for 2 hours. Add soup and green chiles and continue simmering an additional 15-20 minutes, stirring until soup is blended.

Spicy Meatball Burritos

Mamma mia that's a spicy meatball! Try this recipe, if you survive the first time, increase the chili powder. What a kick! Of course you can always start with only half the recommended amount and work your way up!

2 lbs. GROUND BEEF
1 lg. BELL PEPPER, diced
2 med. GARLIC CLOVES, minced
1 lg. ONION, diced
1/4 Tbsp. SALT
4 Tbsp. CHILI POWDER
2 EGGS
1 Tbsp. PARSLEY
1 cup BROWN RICE, pre-cooked for 15 minutes
2 cans (15 oz. each) TOMATO SAUCE
1 cup WATER
1 tsp. CHILI POWDER
6-8 (10-12") FLOUR TORTILLAS

In a large mixing bowl, combine ground beef, bell pepper, garlic, onion, salt, chili powder, eggs, parsley and brown rice. Mix well. Roll into balls the size of a large walnut. Set aside. In a large skillet, add tomato sauce, water and chili powder. Simmer. Add meatballs and continue simmering for 40-50 minutes. Stir occasionally. When done, fill tortillas and serve with your favorite salsa. You may wish to garnish dish with lettuce and tomato.

Makes 5-6 servings.

Taco de Gallina
(Chicken Tacos)

1 med. ONION, chopped
2 Tbsp. BUTTER or MARGARINE
2 cups CHICKEN, cooked and cubed
1 cup CHEDDAR CHEESE, shredded
SALT, to taste
VEGETABLE OIL
12 BUENO® BLUE CORN or CORN TORTILLAS

In a medium size skillet, sauté onion in margarine until translucent. Remove from heat and mix in chicken, cheese and salt. Heat vegetable oil in medium size skillet until hot. Quickly dip tortillas, one at a time, into the hot oil to soften. Do not overcook. Drain on paper towel. Place chicken mixture in each tortilla and roll up tightly. Fasten with toothpick. Place in baking pan and bake at 350° for 15 minutes. Serve with **Bueno Taco Sauce** (below) and a tossed salad.

Serves 6.

Bueno Taco Sauce

1 Tbsp. BUENO® PEQUÍN, crushed
1/2 tsp. GARLIC POWDER
1/2 tsp. SALT
1 tsp. ONION, dehydrated or finely chopped
dash of BUENO® OREGANO
1/4 cup VINEGAR
1 can (16 oz.) TOMATOES, finely chopped
1/3 cup WATER

Combine all ingredients in medium size saucepan and simmer for 20 minutes. Serve hot or cold.

Bueno Burro

1 lb. GROUND BEEF
1/2 cup ONION, chopped
1/3 cup TOMATO PASTE
1/3 cup WATER
dash BUENO® OREGANO
1 1/2 tsp. GARLIC POWDER
1/2 tsp. BUENO® GROUND CUMIN
1 Tbsp. VEGETABLE OIL
1 qt. PINTO BEANS, cooked and drained
1 cup LONGHORN or CHEDDAR CHEESE, grated
1 pkg. (1 doz.) BUENO® WHITE FLOUR TORTILLAS
1 container (13 oz.) BUENO® FROZEN GREEN CHILES

Brown beef in skillet. Add onions and sauté. Blend in tomato paste, water, oregano, garlic powder and cumin. Simmer for 15 minutes. In another skillet, heat vegetable oil. Add beans and simmer until much of the moisture has evaporated. Mash beans and add half of cheese, allowing it to melt. Divide both mixtures among tortillas. Top with desired amount of green chile and cheese. Roll once toward middle, fold over edges and roll again over folded edges. Place each burro seam-side down on a cookie sheet and bake at 325° for 15 minutes until cheese has melted. Eat as is or top with *Bueno Taco Sauce* (see previous page). For a slightly different flavor, fry the burros instead of baking.

Makes 12 burros.

Tostadas de Carne y Cerveza
(Beef & Beer Tostadas)

1 lb. GROUND BEEF
4 GREEN ONIONS, diced
1 can (4 oz.) TOMATO PASTE
1 can (12 oz.) BEER
1 can (4 oz.) GREEN CHILES, diced
1 clove GARLIC, minced
1 Tbsp. CHILI POWDER
1/2 tsp. SUGAR
1 can (16 oz.) REFRIED BEANS
VEGETABLE OIL
8 CORN TORTILLAS
2 cups CHEDDAR CHEESE, shredded
1 head LETTUCE, shredded
2 med. TOMATOES, chopped
2 RIPE AVOCADOS, peeled, seeded and diced

In a large skillet, sauté ground beef and onion. Cook until beef is browned. Drain, if necessary. Add tomato paste, beer, green chiles, garlic, chili powder, and sugar to the beef and onions. Heat until mixture begins to boil, then reduce to simmer. Continue to simmer uncovered for approximately 20-30 minutes, or until thickened, as desired. Let stand. Next, place refried beans in small saucepan and heat.

Heat 1/4 to1/2-inch vegetable oil in small skillet until hot. Dip each tortilla into heated oil. Cook each side for approximately 20-40 seconds, or until crisp and lightly browned. Place on paper towel to drain.

When ready to serve, prepare each tostada separately. Spread generous amount of beans over top of tortillas and layer with meat mixture to cover beans. Sprinkle cheddar cheese over mixture. Add lettuce and tomatoes. Top with avocado and serve warm.

Serves 4.

Happy Coyote Tacos

1 can (15 oz.) BLACK BEANS, drained
1 cup PICANTE SAUCE
1 med. ONION, chopped
1 tsp. GARLIC POWDER
1 cup CORN
8 CORN TORTILLAS
1 pkg. (4 oz.) CREAM CHEESE
LETTUCE, shredded
2 lg. TOMATOES, diced

In a large bowl, mix together black beans, picante sauce, onion, garlic powder, and corn. Set aside. Soften tortillas by placing each in hot oil for a few seconds per side. Drain on paper towels. Spread cream cheese on one half of softened tortilla. Add shredded lettuce and follow with bean mixture. Top with tomatoes and fold remaining half of tortilla over filling.

Serves 4.

Shredded Beef Tacos

1 med. ONION, chopped
VEGETABLE OIL
1 can (8 oz.) TOMATO SAUCE
1/2 tsp. RED PEPPER, ground
1/8 tsp. CUMIN SEED
2 cups cooked BEEF, shredded
12 CORN TORTILLAS
1/2 cup SOUR CREAM
2 RIPE AVOCADOS, peeled, seeded and mashed

In a large skillet, sauté onion in oil until translucent. Add tomato sauce, pepper and cumin seed. Cover and simmer for approximately 5 minutes. Stir in shredded beef and continue to cook until meat is heated through.

Meanwhile, soften tortillas by dipping each one into hot vegetable oil for a few seconds per side. Drain on paper towels. Spoon sour cream and mashed avocado onto one half of tortilla and spread. Add beef mixture. Fold remaining half of tortilla over filling. Serve immediately for a tantalizing treat.

Makes 6 servings.

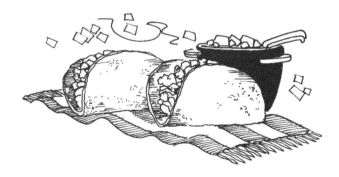

Mexican Pizza

1/4 cup JALAPEÑO PEPPER, seeded and diced
1/2 cup TOMATO, diced
1/4 cup GREEN ONIONS, diced
1/2 cup TURKEY, cooked and diced
1 lg. (10-12") FLOUR TORTILLA
1 cup JACK CHEESE, grated
PEPPER, to taste
SALSA, as desired

Combine jalapeño, tomato, green onions and turkey in bowl and mix. Place flour tortilla on non-stick cookie sheet. Spread cheese generously covering top of tortilla. Top with remaining ingredients. Sprinkle pepper to taste. Broil for approximately 5-10 minutes or until cheese bubbles. Serve with favorite salsa.

Serves 1-2.

Sonoran Beef Casserole

1 lb. GROUND BEEF, lean
1 lg. ONION, diced
1 clove GARLIC, minced
1 can (10 3/4 oz.) CREAM OF MUSHROOM SOUP
8-10 oz. PROCESSED CHEESE, cubed
1 can (7 oz.) diced GREEN CHILES, drained
1 can (12 oz.) EVAPORATED MILK
TORTILLA CHIPS

In a medium skillet, sauté meat, onion and garlic. Meanwhile, in a saucepan, combine soup, cheese, chiles and milk. Heat until cheese is melted. Generously layer tortilla chips in bottom of greased casserole dish. Add meat mixture. Top with melted cheese mixture to complete layers. Bake at 350° for approximately 45 minutes.

Serves 6.

New Mexico Style Tostadas

1 lb. lean GROUND BEEF
3/4 cup GREEN ONIONS, chopped
1 tsp. CHILI POWDER
1 tsp. SALT
2 lg. TOMATOES, diced
1 can (7 oz.) TOMATILLOS, drained
1 can (7 oz.) diced GREEN CHILES, drained
1 can (16 oz.) PINTO BEANS, drained
1 Tbsp. crushed OREGANO
8 CORN TORTILLAS
CANOLA OIL
1 head LETTUCE, shredded
2 cups CHEDDAR CHEESE, shredded

Combine ground beef, green onions, chili powder and salt in large skillet. Sauté until meat is browned, stirring frequently. Drain. Add tomatoes, tomatillos and green chiles to meat mixture. Cook 15 minutes on medium heat, stirring occasionally. Add beans and oregano to mixture and cook an additional 5 minutes.

In a small skillet, heat approximately 1 inch oil on high heat. Place each tortilla in hot oil for about 30 seconds on each side. Drain on paper towels. Spread beef mixture on each tortilla, then the shredded lettuce and top with cheddar cheese.

Serves 8.

Mabel's Magnificent Green Chile Burros

When Mabel throws a party, the whole neighborhood comes. Now you can have great parties, too, by serving this excellent dish. The only catch is you have to invite Mabel!

2 ROUND STEAKS, diced
1 tsp. SALT
1 tsp. CUMIN POWDER
1/2 tsp. BLACK PEPPER
1 lg. ONION, diced
3 cloves GARLIC, diced
1 tsp. GARLIC POWDER
1 can (4 oz.) diced GREEN CHILES, drained
1 jar (16 oz.) JALAPEÑO GREEN SALSA
8-10 (10-12") FLOUR TORTILLAS
FLOUR, as desired

Place all ingredients except chiles, salsa, tortillas and flour in a crockpot. Cook all day, or until meat is tender. Add chiles and salsa 30 minutes before serving. Thicken with flour, if desired.

Warm tortillas and add meat mixture. Fold and serve. Spoon mixture over burros for enchilada style, if desired.

Makes 8-10 burros.

Sherry's Zesty Cheese Enchiladas

1 lb. CHEDDAR CHEESE, grated
2 cans (4 oz. each) GREEN CHILES, chopped
4 GREEN ONIONS, chopped
1 container (16 oz.) SOUR CREAM
chopped OLIVES, optional
8 (10-12") FLOUR TORTILLAS
3 cans (15 oz. each) RED or GREEN ENCHILADA SAUCE

Mix cheese with green chiles, onions, sour cream and olives. Spread in the middle of each tortilla. Roll tortillas and place in a shallow baking dish. Cover with enchilada sauce. Bake in 325° oven for 45 minutes or until bubbly. Serve with sour cream.

Serves 6.

Taco Pie de Acapulco

1 lb. GROUND CHUCK
1 med. ONION, chopped
1 can (10 3/4 oz.) CREAM OF MUSHROOM SOUP
1 can (10 3/4 oz.) CREAM OF CHICKEN SOUP
1/2 cup MILK
1 cup TACO SAUCE
1 can (4 oz.) GREEN CHILES, diced
10-12 CORN TORTILLAS, quartered
2 cups CHEDDAR CHEESE, shredded

In a large skillet, brown meat. Add onion and continue cooking until meat is done and onion is translucent. Drain, if necessary and set aside. Combine soups, milk, taco sauce and green chiles. Mix well. Add to meat mixture. In a large baking casserole, place tortillas on bottom of dish, generously add meat mixture to cover tortillas. Top with a layer of cheese. Continue layering tortillas, meat mixture and cheese until all ingredients are used. Bake in 350° oven for 30 minutes. Serve warm.

Serves 6-8.

Tangy Turkey Tacos

Add more jalapeños for an even spicier taco!

NON-STICK COOKING SPRAY
1 med. ONION, chopped
1 clove GARLIC, minced
1 lb. GROUND TURKEY
2 Tbsp. CHILI POWDER
1 tsp. JALAPEÑO, dried
1 Tbsp. CUMIN
1/2 cup WATER
12 TACO SHELLS
3 med. TOMATOES, chopped
1 cup LETTUCE, shredded
1 cup CHEDDAR or JACK CHEESE, grated

Spray thin coating of non-stick cooking spray in a large skillet. Sauté onion and garlic until onion is translucent. Add turkey and cook over medium heat until meat is browned. Drain meat and return to skillet. Add chili powder, jalapeños, cumin and water to meat mixture. Simmer until water evaporates. Fill each taco shell with 1/2 cup meat mixture. Top with lettuce and tomato. Garnish with cheese.

Serves 6-8.

Old Town Tortilla Bake

In Albuquerque, New Mexico, the center of Old Town is a picturesque area with tall trees, green grass and a bandstand.

1 1/2 lb. LEAN GROUND BEEF
1 med. ONION, chopped
1 can (16 oz.) TOMATOES, diced
1 can (10 oz.) ENCHILADA SAUCE
1/2 cup BLACK OLIVES, chopped
1 tsp. SALT
1/8 tsp. PEPPER
1/4 tsp. GARLIC POWDER
1 EGG
1 cup SMALL CURD COTTAGE CHEESE
1/2 cup JACK CHEESE, shredded
8 (10-12") FLOUR TORTILLAS, cut in half
1/2 cup TORTILLA CHIPS, crushed
1/2 cup CHEDDAR CHEESE, shredded

In a medium skillet, sauté meat and onion. Blend in tomatoes, enchilada sauce, olives, salt, pepper and garlic powder. In a separate bowl, beat egg in with cottage cheese.

Spread 1/3 meat mixture in a greased, 3-qt. casserole. Layer with one-half of Jack cheese and one-half of cottage cheese. Next, layer one-half of tortilla halves. Repeat layers followed by remaining sauce. Top casserole with cheddar cheese. Border with crushed tortilla chips. Bake uncovered at 350° for 20 minutes. Cut into squares and serve.

Serves 6-8.

Guaymas Green Chile Burros

Wonderful restaurants line the sidewalks in Guaymas, Mexico. These burros bring the taste of Mexico to your kitchen.

3 lbs. CHUCK ROAST
3 lbs. PORK
SALT, to taste
4 cloves GARLIC
2 lg. cans GREEN CHILES, diced
3 cloves GARLIC, pressed
1 can (16 oz.) TOMATOES
6 Tbsp. CANOLA OIL
3 Tbsp. FLOUR
10-12 (10-12") FLOUR TORTILLAS

In a large soup kettle, add 1 gallon of water, chuck roast, pork, salt and garlic. Cook (covered) until meat is tender and pulls away from bone. Remove meat from broth and allow to cool. Let broth stand until fat congeals on top. Remove fat and reserve broth. Next, combine chiles, garlic and tomatoes in broth. Let stand while cutting meat into small cubes (about 3/4 inch).

In a large skillet, heat oil. Stir in flour. Continue stirring and slowly add chili-tomato mixture. Add meat and simmer for approximately 15 minutes. For burros, fill tortillas and fold. Serve on plates garnished with shredded lettuce. You may choose to serve this as **green chile stew** with beans and tortillas on the side.

Serves 6-8.

Guadalajara
Enchilada Casserole

1 (1-2 lb.) CHICKEN, whole fryer
SALT, to taste
PEPPER, to taste
GARLIC POWDER, to taste
1 can (10 3/4 oz.) CREAM OF CHICKEN SOUP
1 can (10 3/4 oz.) CREAM OF MUSHROOM SOUP
5 GREEN ONIONS, diced
1 cup BLACK OLIVES, sliced
NON-STICK COOKING SPRAY
12 CORN TORTILLAS, softened
4 WHOLE GREEN CHILES, seeded and sliced
1 cup JACK CHEESE, grated

Season chicken with salt, pepper and garlic salt to taste. Cook, covered with water, in large pot over medium heat until done. Remove chicken from stock and allow to cool. Meanwhile, in a medium saucepan, combine cream of chicken and cream of mushroom soups, onions and black olives. Shred chicken when cooled and add to soup mixture. Stir in 2 cups of the reserved chicken stock to chicken mixture.

Spray casserole dish with non-stick cooking spray. Place a layer of softened tortillas on bottom layer of dish. Next, layer with chicken mixture to cover tortillas and sprinkle with cheese. Arrange a layer of chile slices on top. Repeat layers until all ingredients are used. Bake at 350° for 30 minutes. Serve piping hot and enjoy!

Serves 6.

South-of-the-Border Smothered Burros

1 lb. GROUND BEEF
2 cans (7 oz. each) GREEN CHILE SALSA
1 can (10 3/4 oz.) CREAM OF CHICKEN SOUP
1 can (16 oz.) REFRIED BEANS
12 (10-12") FLOUR TORTILLAS
1/2 lb. JACK CHEESE, grated
1/2 lb. CHEDDAR CHEESE, grated
1 bunch GREEN ONIONS, diced or
    1 cup ONION, chopped

In a large skillet, sauté ground beef. While beef is browning, combine green chile salsa and chicken soup in a medium size saucepan. Heat beans. Meanwhile, soften flour tortillas. Fill tortillas with the following: 1 tablespoon each of meat, salsa mixture and beans. Add onions as desired and top with cheeses. Roll into flute-like shapes and place in casserole dish. Top with remaining salsa mixture and sprinkle with cheese. Bake in 350° oven for approximately 15-20 minutes until bubbly.

Serves 6-8.

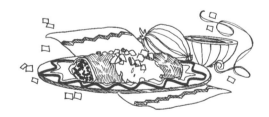

Beef or Chicken Fajitas

For a festive atmosphere serve this meal on a brightly colored tablecloth and add colorful accompaniments such as guacamole and salsa.

Marinade:

   1 Tbsp GARLIC SALT
   1 tsp. CILANTRO, fresh, chopped
   2 tsp. BROWN SUGAR
   1 Tbsp. VEGETABLE OIL
   1/2 tsp. CUMIN, ground
   1/4 cup LIME JUICE
   1 Tbsp. WORCESTERSHIRE SAUCE
   1/2 cup WATER

Combine all ingredients in a glass or plastic bowl. Add **1 pound** of **BEEF** or **CHICKEN** cut into strips and marinate for 1 to 2 hours in the refrigerator.

1 RED BELL PEPPER, cut into strips
1 GREEN BELL PEPPER, cut into strips
1 lg. ONION, cut into strips
1 JALAPEÑO PEPPER, cut into strips
1 can (16 oz.) REFRIED BEANS
1 cup JACK CHEESE grated
1 cup SOUR CREAM
12 (6") FLOUR TORTILLAS

Cook bell peppers, onion and jalapeño pepper in a large skillet or in a wok. Add the marinated meat and continue cooking, stirring constantly, until the meat is done. Heat the beans. Serve your meat mixture right from the skillet or wok. Serve beans, cheese and sour cream in brightly colored dishes along with a plate of warm tortillas. Create fajitas by filling tortillas with desired selections.

Serves 4-6.

Tortilla Treats

Tropical Tortilla Roll-ups

These roll-ups make a delectable dessert or can be used as a light appetizer.

4 (10-12") TORTILLAS
1 pkg. (8 oz.) CREAM CHEESE, softened
CINNAMON, ground
4 KIWI FRUITS, sliced
1 cup PINEAPPLE, diced
2 cups STRAWBERRIES, diced
1 ORANGE, sliced
MINT sprigs

Place tortilla on flat surface. Spread cream cheese, generously covering entire top of each tortilla. Sprinkle tortilla with cinnamon to taste. Arrange kiwi slices to cover 2/3 of the top, leaving bottom 1/3 of tortilla without fruit. Layer pineapple and strawberry over kiwi. Begin rolling fruit-filled tortilla from top to bottom, applying light pressure as you roll. When all tortillas are rolled, let stand five minutes. Slice each tortilla into 6-8 pieces. Arrange on serving dish. Garnish with orange slices and mint.

Peanut Butter & Jelly Tortilla

1 lg. FLOUR TORTILLA
PEANUT BUTTER, to taste
1 tsp. CINNAMON
1 Tbsp. BLACK CHERRY JAM

Lay tortilla on flat surface. Spread peanut butter over entire surface of tortilla. Sprinkle with cinnamon. Spread jam on the upper 2/3 of the tortilla. Start at top of tortilla and roll the tortilla towards bottom, holding firmly in place as you roll. Place in microwave on high for 20 seconds. Eat as you would a burrito. You can vary this treat by adding honey, preserves, fruit, etc. Be careful— the filling may be very hot.

Serves 1.

Cinnamon Crispasnacks

CANOLA OIL
10 (10-12") FLOUR TORTILLAS
1 cup SUGAR
1/8 cup CINNAMON

In a medium skillet, heat enough oil to cover tortillas, 1-2 inches will usually be enough. Cut each tortilla into four wedges and fry until they bubble but do not turn brown. Remove and drain on paper towels. Combine sugar and cinnamon in paper bag. Place wedges in bag and shake until coated. Shake off excess coating and serve warm. Crispasnacks can be stored in a plastic bag or container and refrigerated or frozen.

For a low-fat option, spray baking pan surface with non-stick oil and bake in 400° oven for 8-9 minutes. Coat as above.

For a different taste, try using various seasonings and salts such as ground herbs, and chili and taco mixes.

Pastel de Queso
(Cheese Pastry)

8 oz. RICOTTA CHEESE
3 Tbsp. SUGAR
1 EGG
4 FLOUR TORTILLAS

TOOTHPICKS
2 Tbsp. OIL
FRUIT SAUCE, JAM or JELLY

Mix cheese, sugar and egg in bowl. Place 1/4 of mixture in center of each tortilla, fold in half and close tightly with toothpicks. Fry in oil until browned over medium heat, then cool. Remove toothpicks, cut into halves and serve covered lightly with fruit sauce, jam or jelly.

Serves 8.

Chocolate Tortillas

If you love chocolate and tortillas—this is heaven! Makes a great dessert for both kids and adults.

1/3 cup SUGAR
1 Tbsp. FLOUR
1 Tbsp. CORNSTARCH
1/4 tsp. SALT
1 1/4 cups MILK

1 EGG YOLK, slightly beaten
1 tsp. VANILLA
2/3 cup WHIPPING CREAM
12 (8") FLOUR TORTILLAS

Combine the following ingredients in a medium saucepan: sugar, flour, cornstarch and salt. Gradually stir in milk. Cook over low-medium heat until mixture is bubbly. Continue to cook and stir for a few minutes. Blend in egg yolk, again stirring until bubbly. Add vanilla and cool. When cooled, beat mixture until smooth. Whip cream until peaks form and fold into mixture. Fill each tortilla with approximately 3 Tbsp. of mixture and fold. Place on large platter and refrigerate.

While chilling tortillas, prepare **Chocolate Glaze**.

Serves 6.

Chocolate Glaze

1/3 cup SUGAR
4 tsp. CORNSTARCH
1/2 cup WATER
1 square (1 oz.) UNSWEETENED CHOCOLATE, chopped
SALT, to taste
1 Tbsp. BUTTER or MARGARINE
1/2 tsp. VANILLA

Combine sugar and cornstarch in medium saucepan. Add water, chocolate and salt. As you stir, cook over medium-low heat until thick and bubbly. Add butter or margarine and vanilla to chocolate mixture. Pour hot glaze over **Chocolate Tortillas** and chill until ready to serve.

Blueberry Surprise

1 can (20-24 oz.) BLUEBERRY PIE FILLING
1/2 cup WALNUTS, finely chopped
1/2 tsp. LEMON PEEL, grated
1/2 tsp. VANILLA
6 (8") FLOUR TORTILLAS, softened
1/2 cup BUTTER or MARGARINE, melted
6 Tbsp. fine BREAD CRUMBS
1 Tbsp. SUGAR
1/4 tsp. GROUND CINNAMON

Combine blueberry filling, walnuts, lemon peel and vanilla. Stir gently and put aside. Brush one side of each tortilla with melted butter. Sprinkle a tablespoon of bread crumbs on top of tortilla. Place 1/2 cup of blueberry mixture at top of each tortilla. Starting at top edge, roll each tortilla into flute-like shape. Fold sides under and place tortillas, seam side down, on lightly greased baking pan. Brush each tortilla with melted butter. Combine sugar and cinnamon and sprinkle on top of tortillas. Bake in 400° oven for about 10-15 minutes until tortillas are crispy. Allow to cool for 5 minutes. Cut into bite-size pieces for a scrumptious delight.

For variety, try apple, apricot, cherry, peach, raisin or mincemeat fruit fillings.

Serves 12.

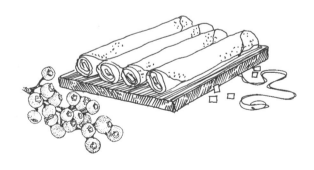

Sonoran Raspberry Rolls

5 (8") FLOUR TORTILLAS, softened
1 pkg. (8 oz.) CREAM CHEESE, softened
1/3 cup TOASTED SLIVERED ALMONDS
Sauce:
   1 pkg. (10 oz.) frozen RED RASPBERRIES, thawed
   CRANBERRY JUICE COCKTAIL, as needed
   1/3 cup SUGAR
   4 tsp. CORNSTARCH
   SALT, to taste
   3 Tbsp. BUTTER or MARGARINE
   2 Tbsp. ORANGE LIQUEUR, if desired
   2 tsp. LEMON JUICE

Spread cream cheese over entire tortilla. Leave a quarter-inch rim around edge. Sprinkle with a few almonds. Roll up into flute-like shapes. Repeat with each tortilla. Save remaining almonds for garnish. Cover and chill tortilla rolls.

To prepare raspberry sauce: Drain berries, reserving syrup. Next, combine cranberry juice with syrup to make 1 1/2 cups. Add sugar, cornstarch and salt to syrup mixture. Heat until bubbly, stirring frequently. Fold in butter, liqueur (if desired), lemon juice and berries. If not serving immediately, chill in refrigerator.

When ready to serve, arrange tortillas in a skillet. Top with hot raspberry sauce, cover, and heat thoroughly. Garnish with remaining almonds and serve.

Serves 5.

Fruit Rolls

1 pkg. (8 oz.) CREAM CHEESE
4 Tbsp. SUGAR
6 oz. PURÉED FRUIT
2 lg. FLOUR TORTILLAS
WATER

In a bowl, whip cream cheese and 3 tablespoons of sugar until smooth. Then add 1 tablespoon of sugar to puréed fruit. Spread a thin coat of the cream cheese mixture on the tortillas. Next, spread 2/3 of the puréed fruit over the cream cheese mix and roll the tortillas. Add a little water to the remaining fruit purée to thin. Coat serving plate with the purée. Slice rolls with a sharp knife and arrange on serving plate. Garnish with fresh fruit or mint sprig. May be stored in freezer.

Serves 4.

Mexican Big Wheels

8 (6") CORN TORTILLAS
2 Tbsp. OIL
8 oz. SEMI-SWEET CHOCOLATE
2 cups SOFTENED ICE CREAM

Fry tortillas in oil until crisp, then pat completely dry and cool. Melt chocolate in double boiler. Dip tortillas in chocolate to coat, place 1/4 cup of ice cream between 2 tortillas. Place in freezer overnight and serve. Makes a great summertime dessert for the kids!

Serves 4.

Chocolate Tortilla Bread Pudding

This is a traditional bread pudding with a tortilla twist.

2 EGGS
1 3/4 cups MILK
1/2 cup SUGAR
1 tsp. NUTMEG
2 Tbsp. BUTTER, softened
1 tsp. CINNAMON
1/4 cup RAISINS
1 Tbsp. VANILLA
1/2 cup SEMI-SWEET CHOCOLATE MINI MORSELS
2 cups STALE BREAD, torn
1 cup FLOUR TORTILLAS, torn

Beat eggs in a large mixing bowl . Add milk, sugar, nutmeg, butter, cinnamon, raisins, vanilla and chocolate morsels and stir. Tear bread and tortillas into small chunks and place in a baking dish. Pour egg mixture over bread mixture. Let stand for fifteen minutes. Place in pre-heated 350° oven for 20-25 minutes, or until done. (Place a knife in center; when it comes out clean, pudding is done.)

Sprinkle additional cinnamon over the top and serve warm with honey on the side.

Serves 4-6.

Index

About the Authors

Bobbi Fischer *is a Registered Nurse and family therapist. Her hobbies include hiking, cooking and eating Mexican food. Originally from Boston, Bobbi fell in love with the Southwest and is now admittedly addicted to Mexican foods.*

Bruce Fischer *is a professional videographer and a native of Phoenix. He has been preparing and serving Mexican dishes for most of his life. Like Bobbi, he too is addicted to Mexican food (but won't admit it.)*

Bruce and Bobbi have co-authored numerous other books including **Cowboy Cook Book, Grand Canyon Cook Book, Utah Cook Book, Western Breakfast and Brunch Recipes, Arizona is for Kids** *and* **Desert Discovery.**

QUICK-N-EASY MEXICAN RECIPES

More than 175 favorite Mexican recipes you can prepare in less than thirty minutes. Traditional items such as tacos, tostadas and enchiladas. Also features easy recipes for salads, soups, breads, desserts and drinks. By Susan K. Bollin.

5 1/2 x 8 1/2—128 pages . . . $6.95

SALSA LOVERS COOK BOOK

More than 180 taste-tempting recipes for salsas that will make every meal a special event! Salsas for salads, appetizers, main dishes and desserts! Put some salsa in your life! More than 230,00 copies in print! By Susan K. Bollin.

5 1/2 x 8 1/2—128 pages . . . $6.95

GRAND CANYON COOK BOOK

Inspired by the beauty of the Grand Canyon, this delicious collection of Southwestern recipes creates a natural wonder in the kitchen, too! Appetizers, beverages, breads, main dishes, desserts and lots more! Includes interesting Canyon facts and history. By Bruce and Bobbi Fischer.

5 1/2 x 8 1/2 — 120 pages . . . $6.95

WHOLLY FRIJOLES!
The Whole Bean Cook Book

Features a wide variety of recipes for salads, main dishes, side dishes and desserts with an emphasis on Southwestern style. Pinto, kidney, garbanzo, black, red and navy beans, you'll find recipes for these and many more! Includes cooking tips and fascinating bean trivia! By Shayne Fischer.

5 1/2 x 8 1/2—112 pages . . . $6.95

WESTERN BREAKFAST and BRUNCH RECIPES

A roundup of hearty western favorites to start your day! Includes ranch-style recipes, Native American and gourmet recipes. Add a western flair to the traditional morning meal!

5 1/2 x 8 1/2—96 pages . . . $7.95

ORDER BLANK

GOLDEN WEST PUBLISHERS

☼ 4113 N. Longview Ave. • Phoenix, AZ 85014

www.goldenwestpublishers.com • **1-800-658-5830** • FAX 602-279-6901

Qty	Title	Price	Amount
	Arizona Cook Book	**6.95**	
	Burrito Lovers Cook Book	**6.95**	
	Chili-Lovers' Cook Book	**6.95**	
	Chip and Dip Lovers Cook Book	**6.95**	
	Cowboy Cartoon Cook Book	**7.95**	
	Cowboy Cook Book	**7.95**	
	Grand Canyon Cook Book	**6.95**	
	Low Fat Mexican Recipes	**6.95**	
	Mexican Family Favorites	**6.95**	
	New Mexico Cook Book	**6.95**	
	Quick-n-Easy Mexican Recipes	**6.95**	
	Real New Mexico Chile	**6.95**	
	Salsa Lovers Cook Book	**6.95**	
	Take This Chile and Stuff It!	**6.95**	
	Tequila Cook Book	**7.95**	
	Texas Cook Book	**6.95**	
	Tortilla Lovers Cook Book	**6.95**	
	Vegi-Mex: Vegetarian Mexican Recipes	**6.95**	
	Western Breakfast and Brunch Recipes	**7.95**	
	Wholly Frijoles! The Whole Bean Cook Book	**6.95**	

Shipping & Handling Add: United States $4.00
Canada & Mexico $6.00—All others $13.00

☐ My Check or Money Order Enclosed

☐ MasterCard ☐ VISA

Total $ _____

(Payable in U.S. funds)

Acct. No. _____ Exp. Date _____

Signature _____

Name _____ Phone _____

Address _____

City/State/Zip _____

Call for a FREE catalog of all of our titles

6/05   **This order blank may be photocopied**   Tortilla Lovers